WHAT YOU DON'T KNOW WILL HURT YOU

WHAT YOU DON'T KNOW WILL HURT YOU

From the Barrooms to the Boardrooms to the Courtrooms

Roger Daley

Ponderosa Press

Reno, Nevada

WHAT YOU DON'T KNOW *WILL* HURT YOU
From the Barrooms to the Boardrooms to the Courtrooms

First Edition

Ponderosa Press
5595 Equity Ave., Suite 500
Reno, Nevada 89502
Phone: 775-335-4725
Fax: 775-335-4740
www.ponderosapress.net
info@ponderosapress.net

Publisher's Cataloging-in-Publication data

Daley, Roger.

    What you don't know will hurt you / Roger Daley. -- 1st ed. -- Reno, Nev. : Ponderosa Press, 2006.

        p. ; cm.
        ISBN-13: 978-0-9771898-4-7
        ISBN-10: 0-9771898-4-8

        1. Success in business. 2. Creative ability in business.
    3. Fortune. 4. Success. 5. Multilevel marketing. 6. Direct selling.
    I. Title.

HF5386 .D35 2006   2005907836
650.1--dc22   0605

Library of Congress Control Number: 2005907836

Book Consultant: Ellen Reid
Book Design: Dotti Albertine

DEDICATION

I would like to dedicate this book to two very important men in my life—Mark Hughes and Larry Thompson. Mark, the founder of Herbalife International, for his vision and dedication. With only a ninth-grade education, he helped Herbalife become one of the largest direct sales companies in the world. Larry, my mentor, for all of his trainings and knowledge based on his own experiences, which I applied every day and became very successful as a result. If not for Herbalife and these two men, I would most certainly still be pumping gas or cleaning carpets.

CONTENTS

FOREWORD

~

About Roger Daley

SOMETIMES WE CALL THEM HEROES. Other times we call them role models, or mentors. It doesn't really matter what we call them. The important thing is that we all have them in our lives. If you're lucky in life, very lucky, you will. For me and countless others, Roger Daley epitomizes all of those descriptions. It's not just about business. It's about life, and how to live it. The following pages take you on an amazing journey. You may not know Roger personally as I do, but by the end of the book you will definitely feel like you do. And if you pay close attention, you too will consider him to be a hero, role model, and mentor!

At eighteen years old, five-foot-three, and 103 pounds, Roger Daley was hardly an intimidating soldier. During his three-year stint in the Army he grew six and a half inches and gained the much needed pounds. However, the military training and experience certainly provided better preparation for the future than his twenty or so years spent sitting on barstools!

So how does a man who was raised by his aunt in the tiny, middle-of-nowhere town of Salineville, Ohio—without the benefit of any formal higher education or business experience—become the founder, Chairman, and CEO of a multimillion-dollar international corporation? How does a man who never earned more than $5 an hour from over fifty-five various jobs become the kind of business innovator who would be nominated three times for the prestigious "Entrepreneur of the Year" award? How does a man with no prior knowledge of our United States legal system successfully fight more than twenty-five lawsuits, greedy unethical business partners, hostile takeover attempts,

< xi >

internal corporate sabotage, corrupt personal attorneys, and corrupt courtrooms and still remain standing, strongly at the helm of one of today's most thriving companies in the health and nutrition industry?

Though more expensive in many ways, the "School of Hard Knocks" often provides the kind of education that a Harvard or Wharton School of Business could never supply. And what occurred at age forty-two would trigger Roger to embark on a journey that would eventually bring him enormous financial, physical, and mental success despite numerous and seemingly insurmountable obstacles. Not to mention the various attempts to destroy not only the business he built but also him and his family personally.

As Roger always says, "The results are the main issue." And in this case the numerous battles fought in barrooms, boardrooms, and courtrooms have resulted in tremendous personal growth, inner strength, and a strong determination to win the war.

The journey continues!

—Mark Nagler, Boca Raton, Florida

PREFACE

~

Confessions of a Bankrupt Carpet Cleaner

THIS IS A TRUE STORY—the reflections of a man who was once a bankrupt carpet cleaner and managed, in his early forties, to turn his life around and achieve a level of success he never imagined. It's a story that if I hadn't lived it I wouldn't have believed it myself!

The story is set in barrooms, boardrooms, and courtrooms. My life's been a wild and improbable ride in which I've held on tight against the odds and obstacles. Time and time again.

Against humble beginnings, dead-end jobs, alcoholism, and bankruptcy.

Against deception, shady lawyers, and unscrupulous business associates and partners.

Even against the injustices of our supposedly fair legal system that can give you your day in court and then mysteriously make a resounding jury verdict in your favor vanish before your very eyes.

Against powerful government agencies that claim to serve the public but in reality spend most of their time deep in the pockets of greedy corporations.

I guess you could call me a survivor. Maybe even a thriver. I never went to college, but I spent a great deal of my life attending the School of Hard Knocks.

Why would you want to hear such a story? Well, for one thing, because my experiences aren't unique. Maybe you grew up poor and disadvantaged and are looking for some hope that your life doesn't have to stay that way. Or maybe you're stuck in a dead-end job, buried in bills, and on the verge of going under. Perhaps you're looking for Opportunity—a way out and up—like the one I found.

< xiii >

Maybe you're already a roaring success in your personal and business life and you just like a good old-fashioned rags-to-riches story that confirms the American dream is still alive and well.

I wrote my story to help people like me. I also wrote it to set the record straight. To tell the truth about what really happened in those barrooms, boardrooms, and courtrooms. This, then, is my own personal testimonial.

To give that testimonial, though, I've got to start where everybody's story starts—back in childhood, where personality is shaped and future struggles are foreshadowed. Or are they?

~

I grew up in Salineville, a tiny town tucked away in a little valley in eastern Ohio. Salineville was so small it didn't even have a jail. It had a main street and two back streets, and your dad could probably call you to dinner from one end of town and you could hear him from the other. That is, if you had a dad.

Salineville was a coal-mining town. Main Street was lined with big maples that in the summertime would leaf out and form a kind of canopy. Driving down the street was like driving through a green tunnel. It's been years since I've been there, but I remember as though it were yesterday.

Salineville was a great place to grow up. People didn't lock their doors because there wasn't any crime. It was like one of those towns you used to see in old movies, the kind of town that presented rural America the way everybody wished it was—lots of shade trees, little white-framed houses with green shutters and picket fences. Friendly neighbors called you by your first name, knew your family history, and really cared about you.

I don't live there anymore. Like a lot of small towns in America, Salineville's fallen on hard times. The stores are boarded up, and the people moved away. All coal mines closed, and the movie theater and the high school are gone. The old folks have their memories; the young people look for jobs where there's a future.

When I started writing this book I lived in Indian Wells, California, a country club village that looks like a resort. I had a custom dream home with all the gadgets. We had a lagoon-type swimming pool and spa, and I even had my own private putting green. We were situated along a magnificent fairway and had a mountain view that could only be described as heaven.

But it wasn't always that way. Not through the first forty years of my life. Through most of those years I was poor, drifting from dead-end job to dead-end job, falling off of barstools and generally making a mess of things.

If you want to understand me, you've got to know where I came from; otherwise you won't believe my story.

Maybe you won't believe it anyway.

But it's true. I've lived it.

ACKNOWLEDGMENTS

~

TO MY SON-IN-LAW MARK NAGLER, who has always believed in me and in my philosophy. You were a significant source of inspiration for writing this book.

My gratitude goes to Aunt Glad, who raised me. I was only seventeen when my mom passed away. Aunt Glad believed in me when I didn't believe in myself.

To my cousin Sally, who believed in me without a shadow of a doubt. You are the best cousin anyone could ever ask for.

Many thanks and love to my sister, Sondra. You did my homework for me and got me through school.

To my friend Tish, thank you for always having honesty and integrity. When times were rough, you shared your beliefs with me so that I could understand. You are a good friend, and it was fun working with you.

To my editor, Leonard Tourney. Thanks for taking the time to meet with me, listening to my bizarre story, and accepting the job fifteen minutes into the conversation. I remember your saying, "No one could ever make this story up. I want the challenge." I also appreciate your driving to wherever I was at the time and having the patience to endure numerous interruptions because of my crazy schedule.

My gratitude is endless to my longtime and good friend Gary Garcia. It is hard to believe that almost thirteen years have passed since we began working together. You have been unbelievably committed, trustworthy, and loyal to not only the company, but also to me personally. You have been in every sense an "unconditional friend,"

< xvii >

and that will never be forgotten. Thanks for sharing this incredible journey with me.

I would especially like to thank two special women who have been a major part of my personal life—Julie Lenton and Jennifer Feldstein. It has been my great fortune to have had them as personal assistants. Julie started with me in the early 1980s, and how lucky I was that she was with me for sixteen years until her retirement. Jennifer has been and still is our very trusted and loyal friend of more than thirty years. She came to our rescue when Julie retired. Neither Barbara nor I could have imagined then that she would still be helping us eight years later. Needless to say, we have been through quite a lot together. I do know one thing for sure—we can always count on her. Thanks, Jen, for your honesty and integrity.

Thank you to the endless list of fantastic people who made this book work. Thanks for your patience—this has been quite a process, and I have learned from each and every one of you.

Special thanks goes to my Book Shepherd, Ellen Reid. Without you, none of this would have been possible. Thank you for putting together what seemed like an endless project. You definitely have surrounded yourself with talented and terrific people. That to me says a lot about you. Thank you for teaching me that there is more to a book than just writing it.

And to my beautiful wife, Barbara. You are my partner and very best friend. In our over thirty-two years together, we've certainly been through a lot. The key to our great marriage is having the utmost respect for each other. Nothing has ever come easy for us, but we are fighters—together. We have never had any help from anyone. We've done everything on our own and with many sacrifices. It's definitely all been worth it. It's a good feeling to know we will spend the rest of our lives together. I love you, Barbara!

Chapter 1

~

Fire and Ice

I WAS BORN AT HOME, delivered by our town's only doctor, who happened to be the same doctor that delivered my mother. We had to do it at home, since the nearest hospital was at least twenty miles off. It was the tail end of the Great Depression, and we lived in what people today call "disadvantaged circumstances."

But, in my early years I never felt discouraged, never felt poor, even though I suppose we were. Heck, I didn't know anything different. My father, who was in the Merchant Marines, set sail for parts unknown when I was two or three, leaving me and my older sister, Sondra, to be raised by our mother. During my childhood we didn't talk about Dad much. He was the man who wasn't there. I wouldn't see him again until I was in my forties, when my wife, Barbara, arranged the meeting because she thought a father and son shouldn't be complete strangers no matter how long it had been. I'm still amazed she was able to find him.

Mom had a bunch of health problems and was virtually an invalid. She spent much of her time in an upstairs bedroom. The house we lived in belonged to Gladwyn Hull, my aunt. Gladwyn is an odd name, and we just called her Aunt Glad. So did everybody else in Salineville. Aunt Glad owned a tiny dress shop on Main Street. She was a single woman and a good woman who took people in when they were needy. Like a mother and father to me, she would live to be ninety-seven, a much-respected figure in our small town and a woman who believed in me long after I had stopped believing in myself.

The house we lived in was a square, two-story affair with a rickety front porch and fading gray shingles for siding. It was an old house

< 1 >

when I was growing up, but most of the houses in Salineville were old. It had been built by my grandfather, who had been an orphan adopted by the Hull family. Aunt Glad, his daughter, had been born and raised there. The house may sound grand with its two stories, but it was really more like a shack.

Yet, I have a lot of good memories of the house. It had a parlor and a living room downstairs along with a smaller dining room and a country kitchen. Upstairs were the three bedrooms, one of which was mine. It's funny how things seem so much bigger when you're a kid. Years later when I returned I couldn't believe how tiny and cramped the place really was. We had a coal furnace but there was no heat upstairs, except what drifted up naturally through the cracks and up the stairwell. We didn't have any hot water upstairs either. Later in my boyhood I used to think the reason I didn't grow faster was that I must have shivered all my energy away just trying to stay warm in those frigid Ohio winters.

The summers were the exact opposite. Hot and sweaty, we kept the windows open twenty-four hours a day. The nights were still unbearable. When I was old enough, I'd crawl out of the window of my room onto the front porch roof and sleep under the stars. Indoor plumbing? That we had, but many of my friends' homes had outhouses.

A GOOD KID, BUT NO ANGEL EITHER

I had a happy childhood despite my parents' divorce, my absentee father and invalid mother, and the fact that we were poor. In those years, who wasn't? Especially in small-town America. I'm supposed to be bad, I guess, because of all that. Sociologists usually consider poverty and the absence of a father a royal road to crime. But that wasn't the way it was with me. I was a good kid really—no angel, but no delinquent either. I attended the Church of Christ with my aunt and sister. I went every Sunday, rain or shine, and every year I'd get a badge for my attendance and every year I went to church camp.

I had a good voice, sang in the choir, and sometimes soloed, both at the Church of Christ and at other churches. We had a piano in the living room that Aunt Glad and my mom could play. We'd all sing together, including my sister, Sondra, who also had a good voice. I played the drums too, but not in church. And not always in the house. Aunt Glad would say she'd be losing her hearing soon enough without my drumming to hurry it along.

We did a lot together as a family. These were the golden years of radio, and the radio became a kind of centerpiece of our home life. We'd listen to great programs such as *Sky King* and *Inner Sanctum* and then imagine together what the characters looked like. We didn't need pictures in those days. Our imaginations did it all.

My uncle, Sid Daley, ran a confectionary store in town and sold homemade ice cream, hamburgers with real meat, and news magazines. He also sold the East Liverpool newspaper, so through much of my boyhood I delivered newspapers and became, I guess, a pretty familiar figure in Salineville. I used to like to deliver to the old people, who seemed to enjoy talking to a scrawny kid patient enough to listen to their stories and complaints. It was a great job. When I was nine, I began paying social security, which was relatively new back then, and felt pretty grown-up in doing it.

When I admit to having been a good church-going kid I don't mean to say I didn't get into trouble. I had household chores I sometimes neglected, and I and my friends sometimes pulled pranks that put gray in Aunt Glad's hair. I cussed and smoked a little, although not in the house, pulled some heavy-duty pranks on Halloween, and got sent to the principal's office on a regular basis.

One time my cousin and I managed to nearly burn down Aunt Glad's barn, which sat at the back of the house where a detached garage might have been had the house not been built in the pre-automobile age. We didn't set the fire on purpose. We were reckless kids, not arsonists. We were smoking out there—almost all us kids smoked in those days—lighting matches and inhaling. We were hiding under a pile of lumber, and my cousin started fooling around with the lighter fluid, squirting it at me and at the wood. Next thing we knew, we'd started a fire. We tried to put it out, but it got out of control. We became plenty scared, then, and crawled through the barn window and ran all the way to the other side of the house.

A fire made quite a show. I guess somebody called the fire department because we could hear the siren screaming behind us. Later we tried to play innocent, but one of the neighbors had seen us crawling through the window and ratted on us.

My aunt whipped me good, but didn't call the police. In those days you handled that kind of delinquency in the home, not in the courts, so I managed to keep a clean record, although my aunt never forgot the incident. I can still feel her sharp slap on my behind.

MY NEAR-DEATH EXPERIENCE

The other thing I'm remembered for in Salineville is having had a brush with death, but that was a number of years before the barn-burning episode.

Back in the early 1990s some of my business buddies went back to Salineville to interview my old neighbors, people whom I grew up with or who were adults at the time and remembered my wild youth. They filmed it all—the streets, the houses, the people. Since it was all done in connection with a planned birthday "roast," my good buddies were looking for historical "dirt"—you know, the kind of stories that you hope no one ever remembers or tells because it's the dumb stuff you do when you're a kid and you've got all the time in the world and about as much good sense as a sheep. I remember one of the interviews—a couple of local kids on bicycles who were asked if they had ever heard of Roger Daley. "Sure," they said without missing a beat, "he's the kid that almost drowned in the creek." Then they pointed down to where the creek still flows as though there's a monument to me right there on the banks, which of course there isn't.

Maybe my buddies told the kids what to say, or maybe the kids really had heard the stories and I had truly become a local legend. Anyway, here's the unvarnished truth.

We had a creek in Salineville that ran through the town. In the summers we swam there. In the winters we skated. A railroad bridge spanned the creek. The junior high school was on one side, the high school on the other.

Anyway, I was about five, and one weekday afternoon I asked my mother if I could go skating down at the creek. Naturally, she said no. The creek was dangerous, she pointed out. A boy could fall and break a leg, or fall through the ice and stay frozen until spring. Just as naturally, I ignored my mom's wise advice and snuck off. I was dressed in a heavy snowsuit and we were having a great time when all of a sudden the ice broke. Before I knew what had happened, I slipped under, headfirst.

Luckily, one of my friends, Joe Keating, had grabbed my foot or I would have been completely out of reach, but the other boys didn't have the strength to pull me up. To this day I can remember struggling for breath and seeing the bubbles floating up toward the surface like a lot of little balloons.

Then everything went black. I didn't see any tunnels of light to walk into or departed relatives waiting to embrace me. At least not that I remember.

There was just a cold, empty blackness.

I awoke in the industrial arts building of the high school, and my uncle, who was a mailman and had been walking his route and seen the commotion down at the creek, was giving me what passed in the early 1940s for artificial respiration—a lot of arm raising, back thumping, and old-fashioned praying.

I do remember opening my eyes and looking up into some faces filled with amazement and relief. Nobody was going to have to tell my mom her little boy had bought the farm.

They tell me I was under the water for thirty or forty seconds—long enough to drown at least. I read somewhere not too long ago that ice-cold water can shut the brain down when you're suddenly submerged in it, making it possible to revive drowned persons who have been under for as long as ten or twenty minutes.

Maybe that's what happened to me. Anyway, the doctor was called, and he checked me out. There was no brain damage—at least not that he could tell—but I did develop a case of double pneumonia that kept me in bed for a week.

There was a big write-up about the incident in the newspaper—not in Salineville, which was too small to have a newspaper—but in East

Liverpool, the nearest "big" town. So at least for a few weeks afterward I was a local celebrity. After all, my near-death experience was probably one of the most exciting things that had ever happened in my hometown.

My mom had some words for me about doing what she told me not to do, but I don't remember what they were. I suppose any parent would have said the same kind of things. Aunt Glad wasn't happy about the episode either, but everyone was relieved that little Roger Daley hadn't drowned.

Especially little Roger Daley.

My near-death experience in the town creek wasn't the only escapade in my youth. The area around Salineville was a wonderland for a kid, better than a modern theme park with its man-made rides and engineered thrills. We had the woods and rolling hills, plenty of abandoned coal mines, and natural swimming holes in the old strip mines. I guess you could say we lived in a state of innocence back then, not worrying about perverts, or kidnappers, or gangs—not thinking much about the bad things that could happen when you fall into holes or got lost in the woods. Nowadays, people seem preoccupied with safety, and maybe we do live in a more dangerous world. We had one cop in town, who sometimes drove drunks home on Saturday night. That was law enforcement, Salineville-style. People governed themselves, trusted each other, and while our freedom wasn't unlimited I don't think many modern kids growing up in the suburbs can match it. After all, I had been the one who had fallen through the ice and had lived to tell about it. So how dangerous could life be anyway?

A HOUSEHOLD OF WOMEN

I lived in a household of women, so I didn't have anyone to show me how to do guy things, but my best friend, Jim Davison, lived up the street. Jim and I were like brothers. We'd sleep over at each other's houses and get into trouble together. It was Jim's dad who taught me to hunt and fish. He'd take us camping in the summertime, and after school each day Jim and I spent hours tramping around the woods, shooting squirrels, rabbits, and sometimes deer.

I had my own small collection of guns I'd bought from saving money from my paper route—a 4.10, 16- and 20-gauge shotguns, and a .22 rifle. I kept them over at Jim's house because Aunt Glad was scared of guns and wouldn't let me keep them in the house.

But she never disapproved of my hunting. We weren't recreational hunters shooting up the woods. We ate what we bagged and enjoyed it too, just as we enjoyed the vegetables Aunt Glad raised in our garden. We ate squirrel and rabbit, grouse and pheasant, and the local streams provided plenty of free fish—bass, crappie, and even snapping turtle. Yes, we ate turtles too, not because we were poor, but because they tasted good, and if you haven't tried turtle meat, you've really missed something.

Salineville was a town friendly to its children. In the wintertime, the back streets were blocked off from what little automobile traffic there was so kids could sled. The football field at the high school would freeze over and we'd ice skate there. During the holidays we'd have these parades that would run the length of Main Street—from the Catholic cemetery at one end of town to the Protestant cemetery at the other. Marching bands, floats, the VFW! Patriotism was big in Salineville. These were the war years and right after, and everybody had a flag poll and an American flag. Folks didn't set the American flag on fire in those days or spit on it to make a political statement. The only political statement we made was the Pledge of Allegiance we recited every day and all knew by heart.

SCHOOL DAYS

Although I hated homework, as a kid I loved school. I was easygoing and popular, but I don't think any of my teachers had a lot of respect for my scholarship. Heck, there wasn't much to respect. I wasn't much of a reader, and my math left a lot to be desired. I don't remember what I learned in history or geography. I did play in the school's marching band, sang solos, and was in several school plays.

I guess in some ways my biggest distinction was my size. For some reason—maybe because of my near-drowning—my growth had slowed down. Up until the time of my accident, I was the same size as every other kid I knew. I was even a little chubby. But after the creek episode it was like I had taken slow-growth hormones. This made life a little difficult for me. As I said, I loved sports, especially basketball, but no one was going to choose me for the starting five when I was eye-level with the other guys' belly buttons, even in a small town like Salineville. Even so, I attended all the games, shouted with the loudest of the fans, and tried to make up in sheer enthusiasm what I lacked in stature.

Because I could sing, my ambition was to be a movie star—or maybe a singer like Frankie Lane, Johnny Ray, or Bing Crosby. My mom had a big collection of LP records and I listened to them all the time. Saturday afternoons at our one and only movie theater filled my imagination with faraway places and life outside Salineville. Big Broadway musicals like *Oklahoma* and *South Pacific* and westerns were my favorites. And the series *Flash Gordon* and *Sergeant Preston of the Yukon*. I used to run home from school to hear them.

SHADOWS OF THINGS TO COME

It was all great and wonderful what the movies showed us about life in the larger world, but there was a downside too. During the war years, we saw newsreels of the war in Europe and the Far East. It all seemed so far away, although there were households in our town that showed the blue star in the window, telling us that not all the pictures on the movie screen were produced on a Hollywood back lot. You could go to war and not come back.

We had air raid drills and blackouts that used to scare me to death when I was a little kid, which is what I was in 1941-45. They'd set off the siren in town, and we'd have to douse the lights. I was afraid of the dark anyway, even in my own room. Then we'd hear men outside talking, and the air raid warden would come by checking our windows to make sure no light was showing. He'd yell or pound on the door if he could see a light and order us to put it out or hide it. That's when I'd really get scared.

As I look back, they seem strange now, the drills. Salineville was so far back in the hills that you could hardly find it on the map, yet we could imagine enemies taking enough interest in us to bomb Main Street.

I guess every small town thinks it's the center of the universe, and maybe it is for the people who live there. But our fears of invasion weren't just paranoia. We had seen the newsreels of German soldiers invading Polish villages, long lines of sunken-cheeked refugees looking half-dead already, and Japanese kamikazes screaming down on American carriers. Every night we listened to the progress of the war on the radio along with our favorite programs, and we prayed on Sunday for victory over our nation's enemies. There was a lot about the war we didn't know and wouldn't know until it was over and the bodies in the concentration and prison camps were discovered, but what we did know was bad enough.

One of my uncles had been at Pearl Harbor on the day it was bombed. He was due to muster out that very day and then war was declared, and he was in for another two years. After the war, he came back to Ohio and opened up an auto repair shop that he operated for thirty years. He lived to be an old man and to see his sons grow up and take over the business.

Not everyone in Salineville who was called into the service was so lucky.

I was a young kid, but all these things somehow told me that in the big world beyond Salineville life was full of as much danger as opportunity.

Chapter 2

~

Cars, Girls, and Least Likely to Succeed

I LEARNED A LOT IN SALINEVILLE, but not necessarily in school. We were way back in the hills, but we had what I guess today you'd call "diversity," even in our little corner of the world. You had the Protestants and the Catholics, for example. Each of them had their own church buildings, cemeteries, funeral parlors, and public celebrations at opposite ends of the town. Among the Protestants you had a half-dozen or more denominations, everything from the high-toned Episcopalians to the Holy Rollers. You had some plain atheists too, and one Jewish man, Mr. Feldman, who owned the junkyard. But we all got along.

As far as race was concerned, we didn't have Hispanics, Vietnamese, Filipinos, or Arabs—but, remember, this was the 1950s. What you had were the town's original families, like my own, most of whom were of English or Scottish descent. And then you had the more recent immigrants—the Poles, the Italians, and lots of Irish. Their presence gave our little town an international flavor. But the kids all went to the same school, learned how to pronounce each other's family names, and everybody got along. I had Irish Catholic kids for friends and used to go to catechism class with my buddies. I wasn't interested in converting; I was just being friendly. Besides, the Catholics had great barbecues and the parish priest was cool. He used to coach baseball and was a great friend to Catholic and non-Catholic alike.

< 11 >

A LESSON IN RACIAL PREJUDICE

There weren't any black families in town, but there was a family named Jones that lived on a farm way out in the country. Jones was a black man with two wives—a black woman and an Italian woman. At least he lived with the two women. Now that I think about it, I'm not sure what legal relationship they had. The three of them had a bunch of kids together, and two of their daughters, Johnnie Mae and Agnes, were my classmates. I never thought of these girls as black or mixed or anything. They were just Johnnie Mae and Agnes, and they grew up to be beautiful girls and great athletes. When I was a little kid they used to come over to our house for lunch sometimes. I knew them all the years I was in school.

In my last year of high school our class traveled by train to Washington, D.C., to see our nation's capital.

The senior class trip was an annual event and, because our school district was poor, students had to pay their own way. We held bake sales and car washes from our first year in high school just to make enough for the big event three years later. Parents would throw in a little too, if they could. Johnnie Mae and Agnes Jones went along because they were our classmates and had worked as hard as anybody to get money for the trip. But when we got to the hotel in Washington where we were to stay, the girls weren't allowed in. The hotel was for whites only, you see. It was 1956 and segregation was still everywhere.

I felt pretty bad about what happened to Johnnie Mae and Agnes in Washington, D.C. I'm sure they felt a whole lot worse. There we were in a city with monuments to Washington, Jefferson, and Lincoln, and two girls who were our friends and classmates couldn't stay at the hotel we were in because they were black.

The school had to refund the money the girls had paid for their accommodations. I don't know where they ended up staying in town, maybe at a hotel for blacks only. That was my first lesson in racial prejudice.

A CAR IN THE FAMILY

Neither my mom nor Aunt Glad ever had a car, so when my sister, Sondra, got married her new husband brought with him the first car ever to be in the family. He had a '52 Dodge, a four-door. It wasn't a great car, but it had all the basics, and I wanted to see myself behind the wheel in the worst possible way. I used to beg my brother-in-law to let me drive it, but of course I didn't know how. So I asked him to teach me to drive.

I don't know how enthusiastic he was about my driving his precious Dodge. Maybe he figured that sooner or later I'd find my way behind the wheel anyway and I was less likely to run into a light pole or a ditch if I had some instruction. So he taught and I learned. I never crashed the car as he probably feared, but I came close a couple of times before mastering the gearshift and the art of parallel parking. I can only imagine what terrors I instilled in Aunt Glad and my mom, who heard about my driving misadventures through the family grapevine.

At sixteen I was still puny, looking more like an eleven- or twelve-year-old than a licensed driver. I'd have to sit on cushions because I still wasn't five feet tall, and otherwise I couldn't see out of the windshield. I'd measure myself every day, hoping to hit five foot and a hundred pounds. I really wanted to drive, you see, but even more I wanted to grow.

A couple of years later I bought a car for myself with money I'd made picking potatoes, another one of my jobs as a kid. It was a '47 Ford, and it was a beauty. The car had belonged to my best buddy at the time, and I paid him the magnificent sum of $75 cash for it. Man, did I love that car! I worked on it every day. It was sleek and shiny and had a sturdy V8 engine I used to gun because I liked the sound of all that power revving up. It had big wide whitewalls on it, and I'd get out there with a Brillo pad and scrub until the whitewalls were white as snow. I didn't know then that I'd spend a lot of my working life fixing cars. But much of what I know about auto mechanics I taught myself tinkering with that Ford.

CHEAP DATES

I always thought the most beautiful girls in the world lived in Salineville (of course, I'd never lived anywhere else), and as much as I loved cars I loved girls more. Despite my very youthful appearance, I dated a lot in high school. I always went out with girls who were shorter than I was. To me, they were always the cutest ones—cheerleader types—so I couldn't complain.

I never went steady with any one girl—at least not for long. Local kids married young, but at fifteen and sixteen I was thinking of fun, not marriage. We didn't do fancy stuff on dates. In Salineville, every date was a cheap date. You had one drugstore, and the county fair. You had the local lovers' lane and a drive-in movie theater outside of East Liverpool.

LEAST LIKELY TO SUCCEED

I graduated from Salineville High School in 1956 along with thirty-seven other students. I was thirty-eighth in my class, rock bottom. I was five-foot-three-inches and weighed 107 pounds. I had yet to start shaving and used to drink milk shakes every day in an effort to bulk out.

And no, I had not been voted the most likely to succeed. With my dismal grades, college was out of the question. Even if kids in my town had aspired to college, which we generally didn't, most of us went to high school, maybe graduated, and then got an 8-to-5 where you worked to pay bills. You got married and had kids. You didn't get ahead. You just tried to stay afloat. That was life in Salineville—and in much of middle America—in the 1950s.

I had no prospects for any kind of decent work, so naturally five of my buddies and I decided to join the military. We drove off to a nearby town where there was a recruiting office, planning to join the Navy and see the world, but when we got there the Navy recruiter was out to lunch.

Which is how I ended up in the Army. The Army recruiter *was* there. I guess he brought his lunch from home.

In those days when you enlisted, the Army gave you a choice of where you wanted to serve. We asked for Germany, only half-believing that the Army would keep its promise. Within a few weeks one of my friends and I were on the train and heading for Fort Hood, Texas, for basic training.

My life outside Salineville had begun at last.

Chapter 3

~

I Join the Army and See the World

LIKE MOST RECRUITS, I hated basic training. Fort Hood was another planet, hot and dry and flat. There were snakes, armadillos, and tarantulas competing for space with the human population.

Plus the locals talked funny. It wasn't that I didn't have an accent myself. Hell, I was a hillbilly from Ohio. But Texas speech, with its drawl and twang, was just different. The Army makes its introduction to military service hard and nasty for a purpose. It wants to turn boys into men, civilians into soldiers. So Fort Hood was a brand-new scene, far away from the tight little community I had grown up in and where I was more than a number. Talk about culture shock. When I was a paperboy in Salineville, my customers used to bake cookies and knit sweaters for me at Christmas. Here in Texas I was practically anonymous, known only by a dog tag hanging around my neck. We all dressed alike and, after our Army haircuts, looked pretty much alike too.

MIRACLES HAPPEN

Military life is too regimented to seem normal to anybody, but I hung in there. My size turned out to be less of a disadvantage than I had thought when I had my Army physical. It was as if this scrawny runt of a boy had been mistakenly stuck in among full-grown adults. Man, I didn't even shave yet. There were guys in my unit who weighed twice what I did. But because I was light and wiry, I could do a whole lot more pushups than some of the taller and meatier guys, and you do

< 17 >

a lot of pushups in basic training. I also did well as a marksman. After all, I had plenty of practice with a rifle in my hunting days back in Ohio.

But something wonderful happened to me during basic training. I had my long-awaited growth spurt! All during my teen years I had been measuring my height and weighing myself, trying to catch up with my friends whose bodies were all on schedule. Now, suddenly, my growth hormones seemed finally to kick into gear. I gained nearly twenty pounds in basic training, and during the next three years in uniform I added another six inches to my height. My shoe size increased from size 6 to size 9. I wouldn't start shaving until I was twenty-five, but at least I looked less like a kid.

How to explain this miracle? Was it the Army with its hard physical discipline and high-caloric food? Or was it merely my body's own unique timing, somehow thrown out of kilter by my icy plunge and near-drowning in the town creek? Who knew? And I didn't care.

I was just glad to be measuring up.

ELVIS AND ME

In high school I dated all the time, but there weren't a whole lot of opportunities for female companionship at Fort Hood. The town nearest to the base was Killeen. Killeen's population then was about ten or twenty thousand, a major metropolis compared to Salineville. I still don't know how many girls were in that town, but there sure weren't enough for the seventeen or eighteen thousand GI's at the base.

I was at Fort Hood when Elvis Presley was drafted and came there for basic training. Boy that was great! I mean you want to talk about getting dates in a small Texas town? All you had to do was tell the girls you were Elvis's roommate and you experienced instant success.

Elvis and I weren't roommates, of course. He didn't even live on the post. But I did see him around. He was a gung-ho soldier, volunteering for everything and making sergeant in a year. And man did he bring the women flooding into that town. The Fort had to put extra guards on the gates just to keep the women out.

I was there for a year before I shipped out. The Army had kept its promise after all. I was on my way to Germany. Actually, so was Elvis, although he took a plane. I didn't.

COLD WAR, COLD BEER

I had missed out on the Navy, but not the sea. Our division was sent to Europe on a merchant ship, and my 36-day voyage was the first time I had seen the ocean. Texas was strange, but it was the weeks on the Atlantic that convinced me I wasn't in Ohio anymore. It was onboard that I realized what the expression "packed like sardines" really meant. The ship rocked and the ship rolled, and I suppose for an Ohio boy I did pretty well holding on to my dinners. A lot of my ship-mates weren't so lucky. The ship reeked of sweat and vomit. The voyage seemed endless.

But Germany was fun. I was stationed at Ulm, a beautiful little Bavarian town between Stuttgart and Munich. I was in a scout platoon for a tank battalion. That meant I spent a lot of time in the field—great for a country boy like me. Then I went to communications school and served as a mail clerk for a while. I made a lot of German friends, learned a little German, and developed a real devotion to the local bev-erage, as I'll explain later.

Europe was a real trip. Travel by train was inexpensive, and since the Army gave me food and lodging I could afford to spend a lot of my basic pay on entertainment. I toured Paris, Austria, Italy. Europe reeked of history, and I loved the food, especially in Italy, where it was plentiful and cheap. I don't mean to say my Army experience was all fun and games. The Cold War was on everybody's mind then. The Berlin Wall had gone up, and we were always ready if the Russians tried any funny business. The threat of a world war was always in our minds and it was reflected in the intensity of our training. For months it seemed we were always on maneuvers.

Yet for all that training, we thankfully never saw combat. We were on a long vacation compared to what soldiers of my father's era expe-rienced in the same part of the world or what my own generation would endure a dozen years later in the jungles and rice patties of Vietnam.

While in the Army, I counted the days until I could get out. I might have been a soldier in uniform, but I was a civilian at heart. Yet looking back after all these years, I remember only the fun times. Besides, if it hadn't been for the Army, I would probably never have made it to Europe, never toured Austrian castles or seen the Eiffel Tower close-up.

Of course, I also may not have developed a taste for German beer.

Chapter 4

~

California, Here I Come

ISAW CALIFORNIA FOR THE FIRST TIME in 1960 when I went to visit an Army buddy who invited me to come out to stay for a few days. "Why not?" I thought. Who didn't want to go west sometime in his life? Besides, it was January and cold in the East, and just because I had grown up in the Snowbelt didn't mean I liked it. My friend lived in Venice, a Los Angeles suburb, but my first view of the Golden State was a town called Needles.

Needles is just across the border from Arizona and if you've never been there—and you probably haven't—you haven't missed a lot. Even the residents sometimes call the town "Needless." When I got there, though, I thought I'd died and gone to heaven. I saw my first palm tree, felt the warmth, and got excited.

When I got out of the Army, I went back to Salineville. It was wintertime, snowing, and miserable. The town hadn't changed much, hardly at all. But I had! For one thing, I was taller and bulkier, so much so that some of my old friends hardly recognized me. For another thing, I was more ambitious. I had left when I was eighteen, a scrawny kid who looked hardly old enough to drive. Now I was twenty-one, a real adult. At eighteen the future means the day after tomorrow. At twenty-one your view is a little more long-term. Besides, while the town itself had not changed, the home front had changed a whole lot. My mother died during my sophomore year in high school. My sister, Sondra, had married and settled in a home of her own. Only Aunt Glad remained in the house on Main Street where I'd grown up, and even she realized how few prospects there were for a returning soldier. I guess Europe had made a difference in the way I saw things too. The

< 21 >

smallness of Salineville that gave me a comfortable start in life now seemed too restrictive. I needed room to grow. So a friend and I were out drinking one night at a local nightspot and I said, "Let's go to California," and he said, "Why not?"

I went home and left a note on the kitchen table telling Aunt Glad of my plans. I probably should have spoken to her directly. I owed it to her after all she had done for me, but I didn't want any argument and thought I could call her once I got to California.

VENICE ADVENTURE

I lived for about six weeks with another Army friend in Venice, California, until I could save up enough for a place of my own. Venice in those years was pretty much what it still is, a funky beachside community of older houses and apartments. It was the middle of January, but everywhere you looked people were decked out in shorts and T-shirts, great tans, and beautiful bodies. I lived in an old motel converted into apartment units. It was only a couple of blocks from the ocean, and if the wind was just right you could walk out my front door and smell the salt air.

I got my first job there as a mail clerk for the Rand Corporation largely because I had experience mail handling in the Army and, most important, I still had my top secret security clearance. That saved my new employers several thousand dollars right off the bat because it meant they didn't have to train and qualify someone else.

It wasn't a bad job as jobs went. I had handled mail in the Army, so knew the procedures, and there really wasn't much to know. The pay was okay too. I was single, without many expenses, and because there were about a thousand secretaries working there the dating possibilities were awesome. Yet I had a hard time making real friends in California. Somebody broke into my apartment and stole a bunch of stuff. I became disillusioned, and after a year I moved back to Salineville. I thought life was better in the small town of my youth, where people knew your name and knew your folks' name. The problem was that the employment picture hadn't improved. The mines had all closed down. So did the pottery, and my old friends from high school were now commuting to distant towns. I spent a month or so catching up with my family, then headed back to the West Coast, feeling like a yo-yo, which pretty much describes the way I was in those days.

MARRIAGE

For the next few years I worked for Bethlehem Steel, Avis, Harvey Aluminum, and Reynolds Aluminum. But I couldn't stay with anything very long. Nothing really fit. I felt like I was running in place, getting older without getting wiser. I certainly wasn't getting any richer. I dated around, had a bunch of girlfriends, and finally in 1964 I married.

My first wife, Libby, was only seventeen when we hooked up, although I got the impression she was older. Maybe that was because she was divorced and had a child. But she was from North Carolina and had gotten married for the first time when she was fifteen. I had just broken up with a girlfriend myself, so we both came together on the rebound, so to speak. It wasn't the greatest start for a marriage. And it turned out not to be a great marriage. Neither of us was ready, I guess, and our personalities and interests clashed right from the start.

My new father-in-law owned Helm's Texaco station in Redondo Beach, and he offered me a job as a mechanic. I took it, and for the next twelve years I changed a lot of oil and did a lot of tune-ups. We lived in the Harbor Hills Government Projects. "The Projects" had been Navy housing during the war and had been refitted for civilian use. They were blocky apartment houses with cement floors, reserved for the working poor, blue-collar stiffs like myself who were living from paycheck to paycheck and could barely come up with the $75 a month rent. Most of the residents were good people; many of them came to California to find gold only to find it was in the banks, not in their pockets.

In the Projects, almost everybody worked, but nobody prospered. I couldn't get ahead. My marriage took a beating—my fault as much as hers. We separated, then reconciled, separated, then reconciled again. Trying to make it work wore both of us out and couldn't have been too good for the kids either (we had two by that time). We probably should have divorced, but Libby had been through that mess once, and I tended to think that once you were in a marriage you were in it for the duration—despite my own parents' experience. I felt like my life was a complete failure.

In 1973, while still working as a mechanic, I got a part-time job as a maintenance repairman working for HUD—the Department of Housing and Urban Development. I used to drive up to Los Angeles on Mondays to repair the damage done by some of the more unruly renters on the weekends. It wasn't a great job. It had about as much future as a snowman in summer. But it helped pay the bills, and in those days I was living from hand to mouth. My father-in-law got the job for me. I guess he could see how things stood money-wise with us. Maybe he thought he could make things smoother in our rocky marriage if the economic pressures were lightened a bit.

It was a nice thought, but you can't take hope to the bank.

Then an opening developed in Palm Springs and I asked for a transfer. I had lived in the L.A. area for a good ten years now, watching the traffic and air quality get worse and the pace of life become more and more grinding. Palm Springs was sitting in the middle of some of the most barren real estate on the planet, but you've got to drive the L.A. freeways on a regular basis to appreciate why Palm Springs appealed to me. Yeah, it was hot as hell in the summer, but it was quiet and you could stand outside and take in a lungful of air without thinking you were committing suicide at the same time. Besides, I kind of liked the desert. You could see one heck of a long way there, and at night there were more stars above you than you could begin to count.

Palm Springs and HUD housing may seem at odds with each other. Palm Springs means luxury to most people, but you've got to remember that even the rich—especially the rich—need somebody to take care of their needs. Fact was that the government had put up a "project" right behind the Dunes Hotel. At the new project I was responsible for maintenance of the buildings and the grounds. I got free rent (a brand-new, three-bedroom apartment!) and a small salary. I made extra money by painting and cleaning apartments when somebody would move out. But I was still living on the edge and feeling at any moment I'd fall into a pit and never get out again.

MY LIFE STARTS UP AGAIN

I met Barbara in Palm Springs—Barbara who would become the love of my life and teach me marriage could be something more than constant fighting. She and her husband were estranged at the time, and Libby and I had once again split, so I suppose our similar situations may have drawn us together. "Misery does love company," Aunt Glad used to say. But it was more than that. I thought she was the most beautiful woman I had ever seen!

Barbara and her two kids lived in an apartment downstairs at the project. Somebody told me I should meet her because she was from Ohio too. So I talked to her a couple of times and was very impressed. Her family was Jewish and somewhat well-off (at least in my eyes), mine Christian and not; she had grown up in the big city, and I was a country boy. Naturally, we hit it off from the first day.

One day she called me to fix her toilet. Isn't that romantic? Man, you can bet I made sure that toilet worked. I was down there for about a week making sure it did.

Later, our divorces final, Barb and I married. Barb had two children from her first marriage and a lot of bills left over. She worked at Hertz Rent-a-Car out at the Palm Springs airport. I had quit HUD and was looking for work. Our witnesses were Barb's fellow workers from Hertz. We had no money to speak of. I didn't own a dress shirt or suit and had to go out to buy one. Barb borrowed a dress from one of her friends. Yet for some reason we were deliriously happy. I felt a new life had begun, despite being unemployed, and despite having a major personal problem I hadn't yet come to terms with.

Chapter 5

~

Drinking Days and Drinking Nights

INEVER DRANK IN SALINEVILLE, at least not while I was growing up. Aunt Glad never touched a drop and wouldn't have liquor in the house. But when I went into the Army everything changed. In the military, drinking is one of the things you do. You're expected to drink and expected to enjoy it. Getting blind drunk isn't a disgrace but rather a way of being one of the guys. So as a young soldier, I merely went with the flow.

Yet I can't entirely blame my drinking on the Army, or on the influence of evil companions. I entered into the habit with too much gusto for that. I didn't like it at first, beer I mean. Then I developed quite a taste for it. Drinking was fun, and it was a kind of relief from the military routine that can wear you down real fast. My buddies and I would go into Killeen and work our way from one bar to the next. There I learned what the expression "blind drunk" really means.

I've been there and done that way too often.

And I continued doing that after I was transferred to Germany.

In Germany, beer drinking was a national pastime. The brew was fine, really fine. I made it my personal mission to sample every brand. It was my favorite recreation, but what began as recreation soon became habit, and then an addiction, although if you had told me I was an alcoholic I would have called you a liar to your face. I felt I could control my drinking. I was sure I could quit anytime I wanted. Besides, alcoholics were people like my dad—old guys who didn't shave, abandoned their wives and children, and were found in the morning sprawling in the gutters on skid row.

< 27 >

AN EMBARRASSING INCIDENT

One night in Salineville (after I was discharged from the Army), I went boozing with some friends. I have no idea how I got home, but Aunt Glad found me unconscious on the front porch the next morning. What a shock to that sweet old woman! Aunt Glad always thought so well of me. All my life she had been my biggest fan. She hadn't realized the military had taught me more than to march and salute, so she was horrified when she saw me there in broad daylight, stinking of booze and vomit—a disgrace to myself and a spectacle to the neighbors.

Horrified and angry, she woke me up and pulled me to my feet. As she helped me into the house she murmured something about my long-lost father, hoping I wouldn't end up like him.

I felt terrible about what Aunt Glad had seen—and even worse about what she said. I had heard stories about my dad over the years, how he was a hard drinker, but I had never been ashamed of him. Rather, I had found him kind of interesting and was pleased when someone would compare me to him in some way. It was a connection with the dad I'd never had. But now I wasn't so pleased and certainly not very proud. I was deeply ashamed of what I had done to my aunt.

Too bad the experience wasn't shameful enough to make a change in my life.

Back in California, I'd get drunk every weekend and some weeknights too. My best friends—and my new in-laws—were my drinking buddies. We'd have family gatherings and get drunk. We'd go fishing and get drunk. We'd go to bars and shoot pool and drink until we couldn't see straight. I'd regularly topple off bar stools and have to be carried out of the place. Drink. That's all we'd do. And it was okay because we all did it and it seemed normal and right to fall off a bar stool.

Was I an alcoholic? Yes, I was. I'd started to drink every night after work, sometimes until two in the morning. Then I'd drink on the job, making sure I had access to enough to carry me until quitting time. Sometimes I'd wake up on some bar stool and not remember where I left my car, or even if I owned a car.

What a waste of time it was! I look back on my life then and it seems like somebody else's, not mine. The truth, though, was that it was mine. My life consisted of crawling from bar to bar on Beacon Street in San Pedro. I was just one step above the derelicts who had given up on even the semblance of a respectable life. The most that could be said for me was that I was still trying to maintain the illusion of respectability—or so I thought.

I continued to drink hard and often after we moved to Palm Springs. I simply found a new set of watering holes and a different group of drinking buddies to join me.

Anyway, I got stopped one night for drunk driving and a judge in San Pedro gave me a choice of jail or AA. That was an easy choice! I went to AA for a while, got sober for six weeks, and then started again big-time when one day I saw my AA sponsor's car parked outside a bar and went in to find him tottering on the bar stool with a bunch of empties in front of him.

I celebrated my discovery of his hypocrisy by tying one on.

After that I was back in the saddle again. I never liked AA anyway. I got tired real fast of listening to all the sanctimonious preaching. It was depressing, all that sitting around drinking coffee, smoking cigarettes, and eating cake. I don't mean to put AA down. I guess it works for some. It just didn't do me any good. I didn't do me any good either.

After a while, even I began to recognize my drinking was a problem that my willpower wasn't going to solve. For one thing, if I had any willpower at all, liquor had short-circuited it. My drinking helped wreck my first marriage, and when I married Barbara I was still going strong. She had her suspicions, of course, but didn't realize the extent of my problem. I wasn't anxious to let her know about that either. Like a lot of drunks, I was pretty good at covering myself. I could hold a lot of liquor before I looked drunk. But you can only do that for so long before people find out, especially if you're sharing a life with somebody.

One night Barb found me really sick after I had tied one on, and she realized my dirty little secret. Another woman might have given up on me right then and there as a hopeless drunk, but Barb, like Aunt Glad, believed in me. If I had a drinking problem, then she was going to help me overcome it. That was her view. She wasn't prepared to throw the baby out with the bath water. Or in my case, the tonic water.

HELP FROM AN UNEXPECTED SOURCE

As it turned out, what finally got me sober wasn't willpower. It was diversion.

I had a friend who was into long-distance running. Betty would run every day. Ten or fifteen miles was nothing to her. Her body was a lean, mean running machine, and I thought, man, I'd love to look like that! Besides, I thought, here's a sport where you can drink all you want and still perform. I mean, I had this image of gorging on pasta and drinking beer (my two favorite things) without limits, and my body sweating off the damage as I ran.

Soon I was working out and running every day. Suddenly, I started replacing beer with water. Water seemed to improve my performance, and beer simply made me feel sluggish. I also started to watch what I was eating before I ran. Who wanted to run with a hangover, or double up with stomach cramps? I stopped smoking. Cold turkey! Smoking and running just didn't seem to go together either. For the first time in my life, I started to think about my body, how it worked, what it needed. I'd always loved sports, and I had competitive instincts. It wasn't long before physical training and running were as compulsive and addictive as my drinking had been.

NOT ALL ADDICTIONS ARE BAD

I liked my new activity so much I began nagging my friends to get started. I'd nag them until they'd get in running shoes and shorts and hit the road with me. I was responsible for the conversion of a good number of couch potatoes into healthy individuals who looked like they couldn't walk a couple of miles without keeling over with cardiac arrest. I didn't know it then, but getting people motivated to become healthier was how I would go on to earn my fortune!

Had I changed one compulsion for another? I guess I had. The difference—and it was a big difference—was that my new habit was good for me. There was no way I could maintain my newfound discipline and swill beer every night. Besides, my running might have been compulsive but it didn't get me into trouble with the law. It didn't do bad stuff to my brain or liver, either. I was getting healthy and loving every minute of it. And best of all, my new habits were strengthening my marriage, not destroying it.

But it wasn't just running that made me sober at last. It was having a little bit of success at a time in my life when I thought I wasn't capable of it.

Chapter 6

~

Bankruptcy

IT WAS MY WIFE, Barb, who gave me some of the best advice I ever got. It was advice she had gotten from her dad. A person never got rich working for somebody else, he told her.

Believe it or not, I'd never heard that before. I mean, in Salineville nobody was talking about business "opportunities." Business in Salineville meant getting work on a farm, or in a steel mill, pottery, or brickyard and then staying with it until you died or retired—whichever came first. Usually death came first. Business in Salineville meant just getting by. Making enough to put food on the table and splurge at the county fair. And, if you were really lucky, maybe enough for a down payment on a used car. That's the way it was where I grew up.

IN BUSINESS FOR MYSELF

Barb and I picked up the kids and moved to Palm Desert, a town just down the road from Palm Springs. I left HUD and gave up the free apartment to take a job with the post office. I'm not sure exactly why since I couldn't stand to sort mail.

While Barbara was working at Hertz, there was a guy there named Jerry Halstead. Jerry made extra bucks by cleaning carpets. He had some equipment and an old Olds station wagon. One day we were shooting the breeze and Jerry asked me if I would be interested in going into the carpet cleaning business with him. He liked me, he said, and he needed some help. "Maybe," I said, not sure I wanted to leap in any new direction, because the one thing you can say about

< 33 >

working at the post office is that it does give you some job security. Hey, you're a government employee, and you've got a uniform and some good benefits. Jerry came out to our house with his equipment to do a demonstration, just to show he was for real, and did a bang-up job cleaning our carpet and upholstery.

I said, "Wow, this is terrific!"

That's how I started to clean carpets.

Jerry and I worked together for a while. He showed me the ropes. You don't have to be a rocket scientist to clean carpets. You've got to be thorough and you have to be straight with your customers, and I think I was both of those. Other than that, it's switch on, switch off, and some good old elbow grease. Then one day Jerry decided to move to San Diego and offered me the business—lock, stock, and barrel. For the first time in my life I was in business for myself.

As it turned out, I loved being my own boss. Not because I loved carpets, but because I loved working for myself. All my life I had taken orders from someone else—from my mother or Aunt Glad, from officers and loud-mouthed sergeants in the Army, from a mob of employers and supervisors in my many jobs. I had always been a good worker, even when I was drinking. I did what I was told like any other "good employee." But I had always been low down in the pecking order, and to suddenly find myself at the top, even in the small potatoes operation of carpet cleaning, was absolutely great!

Barb and I did the business together for eight years. I did the cleaning, she handled the business end and sometimes helped me in the big projects. We developed a long list of commercial customers and some interesting "celebrity" accounts as well. Palm Springs and the surrounding area is a popular resort for the rich and famous, and these folks need their carpets cleaned just like the rest of us. During the years in the business, we cleaned carpets for Frank Sinatra, William Holden, Kirk Douglas, the Galloping Gourmet, and many other stars. We rubbed elbows with the rich and famous—well, maybe not exactly elbows. We didn't get rich but we made a good life for ourselves. Plus I had a good relationship with Barb's kids. My life seemed to be on the rebound at long last. Too bad it wouldn't last that long.

BAD NEWS

In came 1980 and with it one of the worst recessions of the century. It hit us big-time. Our bread and butter wasn't the carpets of the stars. It was the restaurants, hotels, and businesses, and when the economy went sour, ours was the first kind of service they cut back on. I had to lay off my help and lower my prices, even though my expenses were rising.

We thought the recession would just be temporary, so we plowed all our savings back into the business to keep it going. We thought the economy would rebound. But every day that we went to work we lost money. Soon things went from bad to worse, and I was getting desperate. I owed $3,000 in child support to my ex-wife, fell behind on our mortgage payments, and our creditors were threatening to sue. We got daily calls from bill collectors. If you've ever been in that situation, you know it's a living hell. After a while you just stop answering the phone. You start to imagine everyone knows how bad things are with you and they're talking about it behind your back. You begin to feel worse than poor. You feel dishonest, even though rationally you can't figure out why you should. Barb wasn't willing to ask her family for help. She was too proud for that. I had no family to ask.

We applied for food stamps, just to keep food on the table. I was so embarrassed, I wouldn't go into the market unless it was late at night when I thought there probably wouldn't be anyone there we knew. We had taken a long plunge and now hit bottom. I was so depressed Barb got real worried about me.

Bankruptcy seemed to be the only way out.

THE END OF THE LINE

This was a painful decision for me. I had always been taught that bankruptcy was a disgrace. The last resort of a scoundrel who—through his own laziness, dishonesty, or both—crept into the court to beg protection from the creditors he had cheated. In the 1940s and

1950s, when I was growing up, we all believed in the work ethic. A decent life was all hard work, hard work, hard work. That's all we knew. Give a man ten hours of work for eight hours' pay and that's all he needed. And now here I was, a hard worker who had managed to work myself down into nothing.

If there was a low point in my life, this was it.

But when I got to the county courthouse in San Bernardino to file my bankruptcy, there were about 200 people standing in line in front of me. Suddenly I didn't feel so bad. I realized then that bankruptcy wasn't a moral failure. I was part of a crowd—not of losers, but of those unlucky enough to get caught in an economic vice that was squeezing the life out of us.

I wasn't a perpetrator. I was a casualty.

But it was still the end of the line.

Chapter 7

~

Life After Bankruptcy

DESPITE THESE FINANCIAL PROBLEMS, Barb and I were heavily into health and fitness, and this was helping us survive the economic crunch. We were vegetarians at the time and compulsive runners. Real nuts. We were so nutritionally pure, you could hardly stand to be around us. Barb got part-time work on the weekends in a fitness club for $5 an hour and a free membership. I wound up getting a part-time job there too, because even though the bank had taken possession of my business they let me continue to run it on the outside chance I could put it into the black again.

HERBALIFE

It was at the fitness club that I first ran across a product called Herbalife. In a health club, other members become your friends. Why shouldn't they? You're all obsessed with your bodies, and you keep tabs on each other's fitness routines and diets. When somebody tries something and it works, it's big news! Word of mouth goes a long way in a health club.

Basically, the Herbalife plan consisted of two protein powder milk shakes followed by a single meal each day. The plan also included a combination of vitamin and herbal tablets. Herbalife claimed not only to promote good health, but also to reduce unwanted weight and blast cellulite.

At first, I was skeptical. I mean, fad diets and kooky weight-loss programs were written up in all the magazines, and I wasn't the kind

< 37 >

to believe everything I read. I had seen too much for that. It seemed half the country needed to lose weight and was desperately searching for a way to do it.

I had never seen a person lose weight and keep it off, except maybe when they were really sick. Sure, I had seen plenty of people try, but Herbalife seemed to be the real thing. Barb began to take the product. She drank the shakes and took the pills that went with them. She lost seven pounds in one week, and everywhere she went her friends wanted to know how she was doing it.

Barb's not the kind to keep good news to herself, so she shared it.

Neither of us had any experience in sales. I had never liked or trusted sales or salespeople. To me, they were another alien breed who were always trying to sell me something I didn't need or want. I was vulnerable too. Let one of them make eye contact with me in an airport and I was a goner! But suddenly Barb had become a saleswoman. Without even trying, and without even realizing it.

She wouldn't have described herself then as a saleswoman. To her, she was just sharing with friends. But of course that's what salesmanship is about. Barb's a small woman and she thought she needed to lose sixteen pounds.

In no time at all, she did.

Her friends begged to know how.

We told them, and for six weeks we'd send our curious friends to Mark Doyle. Mark was the assistant manager of the spa and the person who sold Herbalife products on the side. We didn't know we could have sold the product ourselves. We must have sent fifty or sixty people to Mark!

One day I went into the spa to put in an order and Mark said, "Why don't you guys sell this stuff yourself?"

"Sell it? Me? Why didn't you tell me?" I said.

"I thought you were happy being a carpet cleaner," Mark said with an expression that told me he was telling the truth.

At that time I didn't know multilevel marketing from a hole in the wall. I'd heard of Amway and Mary Kaye Cosmetics, but those companies don't recruit from auto mechanics or carpet cleaners. Besides, I was never interested in soap or face cream.

So Mark told me all he knew about Herbalife, and it was one of the most important conversations of my life.

I went home and told Barb we were going to be rich.

Barb asked me if I had been smoking something. After all, we were among the down and out. Bankrupts. We were four payments late on the mortgage. The bank had already taken over my business and was threatening to foreclose on the house. Looking back, I can't blame her for thinking her husband had lost his mind.

What had Mark Doyle told me that convinced me that we'd struck gold? Simple. I asked him what I needed to do to sell the product. He said, "You're already doing it. You're using Herbalife and you're talking to people. Keep doing that, and you'll sell." He was right. We were talking to a lot of people, and nobody believed in these products more than we did. After all, Barb had lost sixteen pounds.

"What else?" I asked.

"Well, you need to get a distributor kit."

"A *who*?" I said.

"A distributor kit. It's got some product and booklets and instructions. It'll cost you $29.95."

My heart sank. Here I was, faced with the biggest opportunity of my life, and I didn't have $29.95. But I knew I'd get it. So I drove across town and borrowed the money from my nephew Kim, who was working at a ranch in Palm Springs.

My nephew thought I was crazy maybe or experiencing a midlife crisis. "You're nuts," he said. "It's probably a pyramid scheme. You'll lose your shirt."

"It's only thirty bucks," I said. "And I already lost my shirt."

I drove back to the club and plunked down the money.

Mark Doyle, now my sponsor, explained how Herbalife worked. "Look," he said, "you sell the product and make profit. But you want to get to a supervisor's position as soon as possible."

He was talking about my being a supervisor, while I was still trying to learn what a distributor kit was!

"You see," Mark said, grinning broadly, "if you sell a $100 worth of product, you make $25."

"Wow," I said, "that's twenty-five percent!"

"You betcha," Mark said. "But it gets better if you're a supervisor. If you're a supervisor and you sell $100 to the same person, then you make $50."

Now I was never big in math, but I was smart enough to realize that fifty percent is better than twenty-five, so I said, "So how do I get to be a supervisor?"

"Easy," Mark said. "Well, you gotta do $4,000 sales volume in one month or $2,000 for two months."

Now, remember that I had just filed for bankruptcy. My total declared indebtedness had been $15,000. That may not sound like much to you, but to me it might as well have been $15 million.

So here's this guy talking to me about $4,000 in sales in one month!

In eight years of cleaning carpets, I never made near $4,000 in one month.

"If you sponsor other people into the business like I'm sponsoring you," Mark went on, "you'll do your $4,000."

Call me naive, but Mark made a believer out of me. It wasn't just his confidence and his enthusiasm. It was Barb's results and my own. Barb had used the product and the weight was staying off.

I wasn't overweight. In fact, I had been underweight through most of my adult life. Even during my drinking years I had managed to stay skinny. If you look at the snapshots of me at the time you'll see what I mean. Of course, my daily running and exercise routine left me with little body fat. So I went on Herbalife's weight-gaining program and gained twenty-one pounds in three weeks!

Barb looked at me and said, "Let's go down to Palm Springs and sell this stuff." As I've said, financially, things were desperate. Our bankruptcy and the higher housing costs had forced us to move out of Palm Desert and into a rinky-dink town called Yucca Valley. Yucca Valley was the exact opposite of the Palm Springs area. It was the low-rent district of the high desert, and you would have been lucky to find more than just a few paved roads.

SPREADING THE NEWS

Maybe you've been to Palm Springs. If you have, you know that the picture-perfect streets are lined with upscale boutiques that carry nothing but the best designer clothes. Price is not an object for the well-to-do locals and tourists who shop there. Barb knew that most of these shoppers were of the female persuasion. Women who, like my wife, were probably very interested in losing weight.

I might have had the enthusiasm, but Barb had the plan. She'd go into a dress shop, pull a size 6 or 7 off the rack, try it on, and come out through the swinging doors of the dressing room complaining, "My God, nothing fits anymore, I've lost so much weight."

All of this was true. Barbara really had lost sixteen pounds, and she was slim to begin with! Now she had a figure a high school cheerleader would have died for. Her complaints got a lot of attention. Every woman in the place attacked! Naturally she was happy to share the good news about how Herbalife had worked for her.

We got money from total strangers. They were begging us for the product.

In our first day of sales we made over $240—more money than I had ever cleared in one day cleaning carpet. After all, cleaning carpet I had chemicals, a truck, help, and gas to pay for. With Herbalife I had no overhead!

Remember, I didn't have any money to buy the product we were selling. We were flat broke. So what I had to do was take orders—and the money—then find Mark and buy the product from him. I left Barb in the stores as security for my return—my new customers knew I'd be back. Poor Barb, sales strategist and hostage all in one day!

The next day, we were going to go back to the carpet cleaning business when Barb said, "I don't want to go back."

I thought about carpet cleaning. It had been my livelihood for eight years and had given me my first taste of working for myself. I was grateful for all that, but something told me my future lay in a different direction. I said, "Me neither."

We never went back. We'd come to a fork in the road. The road sign said, "This way to success!"

Barbara and Roger Daley on cover of *Herbalife Journal*, June 1983

Chapter 8

~

Surprised by Success

ONE OF THE VERY FIRST PEOPLE I RECRUITED as an Herbalife distributor was my doctor, who lived in Laguna Hills and had helped me deal with my allergies. He was into health and nutrition and got excited about the product. He wrote out a check for $4,000-worth of product right on the spot. His first month of sales grossed $13,000! All of a sudden, I was a supervisor.

My head was spinning. I had held close to fifty or sixty penny-ante jobs in my life where opportunity largely meant looking forward to my next paycheck. But I had never seen anything like this. I was forty-two years old, and this was a new world. It wasn't just the money. It was the excitement. Hey, I was talking to people, feeling good about myself and about what I was selling. I had no qualms about what I was doing, because I had seen the future and the future was Herbalife.

My doctor was an exception as far as the typical Herbalife recruit was concerned. He had a successful medical practice, and he was pretty well-off. My typical contact was a person more like me. I went to gas stations, beauty shops, and restaurants. I talked to people with no money and frustrated dreams. I wanted to tell everyone about this great thing I had discovered! I had made supervisor but without having to put a dollar of my own money into the process, and that was part of my excitement. From that moment on and to this very day, when someone tells me that they have no money, I say, "Is that an excuse, or are you ready to go to work?" I'm living proof that you don't need money to do this business.

< 43 >

I NEVER WANTED TO BE A SALESMAN

My first Herbalife opportunity meeting was in a room in the Palm Desert Public Library. My sponsor, Mark, said he'd conduct the meeting and let me be the sponsor to everyone who signed up. My job was inviting the prospects. "What a deal!" I thought. I must have invited over 200 people, but when I got to the meeting Mark had only set up about a dozen chairs.

"What's the deal?" I asked. I told him how many people I had invited, how many had promised to show up. He told me I'd be lucky to see a tenth of that.

He was right.

Mark had set up one chair too many. Eleven people showed up. That was my audience.

I felt like somebody had pricked my balloon. After all those contacts, all those promises—and this! I felt disappointed and betrayed. But Mark kept smiling. You need to know that he was a big guy, a good six-foot-five and a bodybuilder. He was the picture of health and confidence, and because he had been in the nutrition game for years, he knew the science. He talked about vitamins, minerals, amino acids. Amino acids? I'd never even heard of them.

Then Mark's sponsor, a woman named Michele, got up and tried to explain the marketing plan. She talked very fast, drawing circles and squares. That was even worse. To me it was all Japanese geometry, nothing I'd ever learned in Salineville or in the Army and certainly not cleaning carpets. The rest of the folks there seemed similarly lost, their eyes glazed over. Like me, they were looking for an exciting business opportunity, not a boring lecture on chemistry or economics. Miraculously, some of them bought product anyway.

The weirdest thing was I never thought I had any talent for sales. During my first months with Herbalife, I held some of these opportunity meetings in my home. I was a lousy public speaker. I was used to working with my hands, not with my mouth. My first meeting I stared at my feet, listened to my knees knocking together, and wondered if I was going to die or just throw up. And then on top of everything else, disaster struck. The bulb in the projector I had found in a pawnshop burned out, and I couldn't rely on company slides and film clips to help explain the Herbalife program.

I was on my own.

I don't remember now exactly what I said that night. I was sweating like a pig, all the faces in the audience looked skeptical, and hearing myself stumble through an account of my own experience, which must have been repetitive and unconnected, was agonizing even to me.

I did make it through though. And I learned something very important that night. I learned that I was not the issue. The results were the issue. I was just the messenger. After that, the more meetings I did, the more confident I got.

We spoke to all our relatives about Herbalife. They thought we were nuts. We contacted strangers and ended up making friends. But our problems weren't over yet. We needed to buy another car and we didn't have the cash for more than a down payment. This meant a credit purchase, and that isn't easy to manage when you've just declared bankruptcy.

We found the car we wanted and the dealer ran a credit check. That's when we got more bad news. We discovered we owed the IRS for the last two years.

Now I wasn't a tax avoider. I had paid my accountants good money to prepare and file returns. But they hadn't filed. Fortunately, we were able to negotiate with the IRS and make payments, but this was only possible because now we were receiving income from Herbalife.

During those months Barb and I worked our butts off, and we worked as a team. We were holding parties in our home every day, sometimes jamming fifty or sixty people in our living room at one time. We hadn't found a pot of gold at the end of the rainbow, but we had found an opportunity to work. And work hard we did. We worked eight or more hours a day seven days a week. I didn't focus on the money. That was a distraction. I wasn't just selling weight loss. I was selling the opportunity.

And I loved what I was selling.

I HIT THE ROAD

Barb had sent a distributor's kit to her sister, Judy, in Marietta, Georgia. Her sister started losing weight and became enthusiastic about the program. Judy wanted me to come to Marietta to do a meeting. She said she could promise a roomful of interested customers.

Barb was against the trip, pointing out that while money was starting to come in, we needed it to live on. Besides, by that time if I hadn't become skeptical in accepting people's promises to show up for meetings, Barb had. She pointed out that her sister's "interested customers" might be more wishful thinking than reality.

But Barb's sister kept begging, and I finally decided to make the trip. Mark Doyle offered to go with me. Our transportation? Not the friendly skies of United or another airline. No, we drove in an old Pinto station wagon without reclining seats or a lot of rubber on the tires. I don't know how we made it.

Talk about disappointments! For all the promises, when we got there only four people had shown up for the meeting and while all four bought the product we still felt the trip was a bust. But we decided that we weren't going to come back empty-handed. We went out to shopping malls, beauty shops, and chiropractors' offices. We talked to anyone and everyone who would listen. In the eight days we were there we had signed up fifty-one new distributors!

We weren't always that successful. When I made those first trips around the country (usually in the beat-up Pinto), we barely had money for gas. We had to sell product for food and gas money. Forget hotels, we'd sleep in people's houses, often on sofas or on the floor (I had brought my sleeping bag with me). Sometimes we even slept in the car. If somebody didn't offer us dinner, we didn't eat. It was as simple as that.

Then Barb's father, "Arky," got interested in the business (not all of our relatives thought we were crazy). Arky wanted us to come to Youngstown, Ohio, and introduce Herbalife there. This was the middle of winter, with windchill factors well below zero. Remember, this was one of the reasons I left Ohio in the first place.

At that time, Youngstown had been hit really hard by the recession. The city had the highest unemployment numbers in the country. We put an ad in the paper and were deluged with responses. We were there two days and got 400 calls!

We signed up a lot of people, but that fell apart as soon as we left. I was learning an important lesson the hard way. It wasn't enough to generate enthusiasm and get people to sign on the dotted line and become distributors. That was the easy part. You needed to teach people how to teach each other. You just couldn't do everything for them, and that's what we were doing. We were doing the meetings. We were making the contacts. We were providing the energy. In short, we were doing for our recruits what they ultimately had to learn to do for themselves.

Meanwhile, back on the home front I was getting plenty of help. At first our kids were very doubtful about the whole enterprise. When we got our first override check (that's the royalty on our downline supervisors' sales), it was only $200. Our daughter, Lisa, eyed me skeptically and said, "Dad, you're working awfully hard for $200." And I said, "Lisa, you don't understand. We're going to get lots and lots more."

Lisa went to Barb and told her, "Dad's nuts. This isn't going to work."

But work it did, and Lisa soon learned that what I said was true. The next month's check was $600. Then it jumped to $1,300 and then to $2,100. That check made even Lisa a believer. But it got even better. The next month the override was up to $5,200, then $7,200. By May of 1982 our override for that month alone was $21,000. That was in addition to the retail and wholesale profits we were earning.

After years of struggling against poverty, we were absolutely beside ourselves, and Lisa the skeptic was now selling product to her school friends!

These were amazing days and we were all dizzy with success. It had been like a supercharged elevator, rushing us from the basement of bankruptcy to the penthouse of wealth in what seemed only a few seconds. Well, it had been more than seconds. It had been about a year. Even so, it had been one heck of a ride!

THE TOP OF THE HEAP

I had been poor all my life, and now suddenly I had money coming in by the bucketfuls. By the end of our first year with Herbalife we were the highest-grossing distributors in the company, drawing sometimes as high as $70,000 a month in royalties plus bonuses and retail and wholesale profits. Some months we topped $100,000 in bonuses alone!

I guess it went to our heads. I had scrimped all my life, counted pennies and nickels. Suddenly I had more money coming in than I knew what to do with. Naturally, we did what most people in our situation do. We spent it as fast as it came in. We bought cars, jewelry, furs, anything. We ate at the most expensive restaurants and picked up the tab for our friends. We had one helluva Christmas. It was spend, spend, spend. Forget about investing or saving for a rainy day. There's an art to handling sudden wealth. The problem is that rarely do people who suddenly get rich have the art. Why should they? Life's hardly given them anything to practice on. Think about twenty-year-old athletes who become millionaires overnight. Such great wealth is difficult to manage. Heck, I was forty-two and I still didn't have a clue.

The next year we got caught up in the popularity/prosperity ego trip. We started doing meetings for 500–600 people—me, who used to hate the very thought of public speaking, only now I was so super confident you couldn't shut me up. Bill Infante, another successful Herbalife distributor, and I were traveling all over, seduced by all the attention. By now my success had been big news in the Herbalife magazine. Barb and I had been on the front page and we were regularly cited as prime examples of an Herbalife "rags-to-riches" story. We were celebrities and people wanted to meet us, hoping that maybe our magic would rub off on them.

The problem with becoming a celebrity is that you start believing in your own press releases. You not only come to believe you're hot stuff, you become convinced you're indispensable and superior to everyone else. You become arrogant.

Larry Thompson, Vice President of Herbalife and my mentor in the company, had been talking to Barb about my arrogant ways, but I wouldn't listen—either to Larry or to Barb, who was also concerned. After all, I was earning over $100,000 a month. I had a big bank account to prove I was right about things. You couldn't tell me anything. My income was growing by leaps and bounds. Unfortunately, I wasn't growing at all.

Then I went to Sacramento to conduct a large meeting for a distributor who was not in my organization. An audience of about 1,500 people was eager to hear about the opportunities with Herbalife. Before the meeting began, Barb asked me how many of those 1,500 I would be signing up and how many of them were from my downline. (Later I found out Larry had put her up to it.) I looked out over the crowd. Suddenly I realized the answer was none! None of these folks would be signed up into my organization. I was talking the talk, but was no longer walking the walk. I wasn't sponsoring anyone, and my override checks had begun to fall off.

But that realization wasn't enough to set me back on track. After the meeting, Bill and I got together and made a long list of things we thought were wrong with Herbalife, how things were run and how they could be made better. We had big ideas, big plans, big heads. So we set up a meeting with Larry Thompson at his house.

We spent an hour with Larry but the meeting turned out not to be about what was wrong with the company, but what was wrong with us. Larry nailed us good. He kicked our butts for being stupid, for not listening to anybody but ourselves. He beat on us for about an hour but really straightened us out. We left with our heads hanging low, our "list" in my back pocket. I never even had a chance to take it out.

After that I got back on track, remembering what the Herbalife program was about. Most importantly, I remembered that I was not the issue.

Roger Daley and Mark Hughes: Maui, Hawaii, Mark's private beach

Mark Hughes and Roger Daley, Rounder Herbalife International cruise to Tahiti, Millionaire team trip

Roger Daley with Larry Thompson (mentor), Vice President, Herbalife

HERBALIFE "LIFE"

Mark Hughes: Roger's favorite picture

Chapter 9

~

Riding High with Herbalife

I WAS BACK ON TRACK, building my business and working my butt off for Herbalife. The hard work was paying off handsomely. The royalty checks were rolling in, the company bonuses were generous, and the whole family was healthy because we were using the product. Yet psychologically I was wearing myself thin. Barb thought I needed a break. So did Larry Thompson, my mentor. Larry said, "Take a few weeks off. Don't even talk about Herbalife."

That wasn't so easy to do. I had been talking non-stop about Herbalife ever since I had seen what the products had done for Barb and me. They had literally changed our lives. My desire to share the word with others wasn't just about making money. It was about making friends and changing their lives too. Plus, my self-esteem was growing as much as my income. I no longer thought of myself as a bankrupt carpet cleaner. I was winning awards. I was a much-sought-after trainer and public speaker. I wasn't sure that I was prepared to take a vacation from all that.

But when your wife and your mentor tell you to do something, you should listen.

So the family and I made plans to go to Hawaii. You know, sunshine, beaches, quiet lagoons, all the touristy stuff. We had made all the arrangements, booked our flights and accommodations. Then fate stepped in. A big storm hit the islands and blew down the hotel where we had reservations.

I'm not superstitious, but this made me think. Was somebody trying to tell me something? Maybe Hawaii wasn't such a great idea after all. Barb and I were thinking of an alternative vacation when I got a

< 51 >

call from an Herbalife distributor in Florida. He said, "Hey, there's a place down here where nobody'll bother you. It's called New Smyrna Beach."

THE INVASION OF FLORIDA

I'd been in the South before, but not in Florida, and I had never heard of New Smyrna Beach. It turned out to be on the East Coast, in the northern part of the state, not far from Daytona. It was mostly a retirement community of "snowbirds"—people from New York and New England who had moved south to avoid winter. So we took our kids, Billy and Lisa, and a couple of my kids from my first marriage and rented a place on the beach.

New Smyrna was quiet, just as the distributor had said, and pretty. But we weren't there for a week before the kids came banging on the door with a white-haired gentleman and his wife in tow. They said, "Hey, Dad. These people want to know about Herbalife."

I guess my kids told the neighbors what we did for a living, and that had aroused their curiosity.

So much for our vacation from business.

After a couple of weeks of Florida sunshine we returned to California. But I had not only felt the Florida sunshine. I had seen the light! Back at home, I told Larry Thompson about Florida, and he suggested I go there for a few months and open things up. I was gung ho! Why not, I thought. I loved to travel anyway. Every time I had packed my bags and hit the road, we built business. There are no distractions when you're away from home. You've got to keep your mind on business. I'd stayed in cheap motels or slept on sofas in private homes if I'd had to, but I'd always managed to make the trip worthwhile. I'd spent time in Atlanta, Salt Lake City, Chicago, and Detroit lining up distributors, training, and talking to people. Every place I went I built the business.

"Where in Florida?" I asked Larry.

"Orlando," he said.

"Why Orlando?"

"Because it's in the center of the state. You can get anywhere from there."

I checked with all my supervisors to see if any of them wanted to go with me. Twelve said they were game. So Larry came up to my place to talk to them, wowed them with his fancy car, and got them all fired up. "This is cool," I thought. All these distributors were in my down-line, people I'd recruited, which meant I'd get paid on whatever business they generated. I imagined us as the hard core of what would eventually be a small army of distributors, building business from one end of Florida to the other.

Bill and I went first to find a place for the group to live. We knew it wouldn't be easy. We didn't know the place and we had no local contacts, but through the help of a realtor we finally found a four-bedroom house for the women and a big place for the guys not far away. We figured we could use it for meetings as well as living accommodations. Before we all left for Florida, Larry had told the group that nobody would be holding their hands. They'd all have to look for business for themselves.

But it didn't turn out quite the way I'd thought. We weren't there but a few days before some of the women started complaining because the house we'd rented for them was so far from the mall. The complaining got worse and started to depress all of us. Finally, I called Larry and gave him the lowdown. He said, "Buy a ticket for the complainers and send 'em home."

So I went over to their house for a meeting with them and ended up arranging for four of the women to go back. I don't think they were very happy about my little invitation, but they were miserable. I figured they could be as miserable in California as they were in Florida. We didn't need the distraction of complainers.

After that, the work went pretty smooth. The way we worked was this: everybody was on his own to find business. We hit barber and beauty shops, supermarkets, cafes, service stations, and the mall—wherever we could get anybody to listen to our story. And they did listen. We invited folks to come to meetings in the house where the men were staying because we had a bigger living room. I liked the home environment for meetings because we were not only getting the word out about Herbalife but also modeling the kind of meetings our new distributors might have in their own homes. Not everyone can afford to rent a concert hall, but anyone could hold a meeting in his or her living room, even if you lived in a one-bedroom apartment or mobile home.

Things were going well enough in Florida for me to consider moving there. I talked things over with Barb and she agreed. So we rented our Yucca Valley house out to our gardener and his family, and Barb and the kids came down to Orlando. We lived there for two years.

Herbalife had become a household word, and it seemed everybody wanted a piece of the action.

THINGS CHANGE

In 1984 I moved the family and myself back to California. We sold our place in Yucca Valley and bought a house in Palos Verdes.

Palos Verdes was only about five miles from where I used to live in the government projects in southern Los Angeles, but it could have been a different planet. Palos Verdes is elevated above the L.A. basin on rolling hills. It's the ultra-exclusive home of lawyers and doctors, bankers and business executives. They live in big houses with swimming pools, gorgeous lawns, horse paddocks, and great views of the Pacific. Just a few years earlier when I used to work at Texaco as a mechanic I would return customers' Mercedes and Jaguars to their big houses in Palos Verdes and drool. I don't think I ever imagined then that within a few years I could afford to live there myself.

When I went to look for a house, the real estate lady asked me how much I wanted to pay. I said $4,000–$5,000 a month. She looked impressed. Then she asked me if I knew the area.

"Sure," I said. "I worked not far from here for about twelve years."

"Where?" she asked.

"Helm's Texaco."

Her jaw fell. She looked at me as though I was trying to put her on or something. "What kind of business are you in now?" she said.

"Herbalife," I said.

Now that impressed her. I could tell she had heard of the company.

Barb and the kids weren't there when I picked out the house. They saw it for the first time at night. It was a big, sprawling place with what realtors call great "curb appeal"; at night it lit up like a palace.

The kids didn't like the new house at first. We'd always lived in pretty modest houses, even when things started to heat up with Herbalife. They said it looked too much like a hotel.

They got used to it though—the swimming pool, the big lawn, the big cars in the big garage. We all got used to it, even though every day I reflected on just how far I had come from Salineville, Ohio, and how far I had come from the government housing projects, just a few miles down the road.

But things change—sometimes for the better, sometimes for the worse.

Chapter 10

~

Swimming with Sharks

IN 1985, HERBALIFE WAS JUST FIVE YEARS OLD, but it had annual sales of $500 million, more than a million people were using the product, and everywhere you looked you saw the company slogan, "Lose weight now/Ask me how." Everywhere—on T-shirts, on lapel buttons, on bumper stickers. The company had over 800,000 independent distributors selling Herbalife products and sharing the opportunity with their friends and family. Herbalife was now the largest distributor of weight-loss products and vitamin and nutritional supplements in the country. They had a 14-story corporate office building in Los Angeles, and had three distribution centers in California and two each in Georgia, Indiana, and Texas. The company had also begun to develop an international market.

During this time, like Herbalife, I was flying high. We were now in our third year with the company and money was pouring in each month from commissions, royalties, and bonuses. So much so, I hardly knew what to do with it. If I had known then what I know now, I would have saved some for a rainy day. Even in sunny California, sooner or later it rains. You could have warned me then, but I wouldn't have listened.

AUSTRALIA HERE I COME

About that time Herbalife was extending its operations to other countries, and they had recently opened up Australia. Because of my sales volume, I was one of a number of Herbalife distributors to

< 57 >

qualify to fly to Australia at company expense to train newly recruited distributors. Tish Rochin, Larry Thompson's sister, was a former Caltrans truck driver turned Herbalife distributor. She and I worked together a lot. Spunky and outspoken, Tish had energy and enthusiasm to spare, and we were doing training meetings for new distributors.

I loved Australia. We worked every day, doing much the same thing we had done in the States. I found a little family-owned Italian restaurant near our hotel in Sidney and used to drag everybody there practically every night. The Australians were friendly and open-minded. They liked Americans and the things we produced. Mark Hughes, the president of Herbalife, came to Australia to do a big kick-off meeting at the Sidney Opera House. Then Mark's wife got sick and she went home, Mark with her. Rather than cancel the meeting, Larry Thompson, who was along on the trip too, asked Tish and me to sub-stitute for Mark.

"Me in the Sidney Opera House?" I said, feeling a panic attack coming on.

"Somebody's gotta," Larry said. "We have people coming in who want to hear about Herbalife. They don't want to sit staring at a blank stage and listening to elevator music. You call Tish and ask her to give you a hand."

"She's *your* sister," I said.

"*You* call her," Larry said.

And I did. It took some persuading.

Now, the Sidney Opera House is one of the most spectacular build-ings in the world, and Larry and Mark had been expecting an audience of 4,000–5,000 potential distributors. By this time I was a pretty good public speaker (at least when I was talking about what I knew), and yet both Tish and I were pretty nervous about the assignment.

As we were introduced, Tish and I walked out on the stage together. She took about three steps and caught her heel in the floor. That drew quite a few laughs. We got a lot more laughter when I had to get down on my hands and knees to get her heel free. It wasn't a great beginning, but it did a lot to emphasize our image as down-home types, not slick business tycoons. I mean there was Tish, sticking her chewing gum behind her ear and talking like the trucker she used to be, and me as a country boy without a business school education. The message was clear: If we could make money in Herbalife, then anybody who was willing to get off their duff and spread the word could do the same.

We did our thing, and then answered questions from the audience. In all, it was a great meeting, and it would have been a great trip if only the events back in America hadn't happened that same day.

WHO SAID LIFE WAS GOING TO BE EASY?

The next day I was watching the news in the hotel room when I heard the word "Herbalife." Suddenly, I was all ears. I stared at the screen in disbelief. The story was about a lawsuit against the company. An elderly woman living in Florida had died. She had been using Herbalife products a few months before her death, and her children had blamed the product.

Talk about swallowing your heart. Man, I had visions of the company going down like the *Titanic*, but not because these accusations were true. I mean, I could tell by the sound of the story that it likely wasn't. Millions of people had been taking Herbalife products since the company had been founded five years earlier. My own family had been using the product since the beginning and had gotten super healthy. Not only that, but the ingredients themselves—herbs and vitamins—hadn't been concocted in some laboratory out of mystery chemicals. They were natural ingredients. They had been used for thousands of years. Was this solitary, accidental death supposedly caused by a protein shake going to contradict the actual experience of millions of users?

MEDIA FEEDING FRENZY

I knew the company was heading for trouble. The media thrives on disaster. Disaster provides them with pictures at eleven, creates drama and suspense, and boosts ratings. But it wasn't just the lawsuit and the FDA investigation that came later. It was the likelihood that the media would treat these allegations as proven facts. Even before Herbalife had a chance to speak for itself. I knew people wouldn't understand the word "alleged." All they'd hear was "death" and "Herbalife."

Using typical media math, they'd put two and two together and get five.

Right away we got on the phone and began calling our distributors back home. They told us the story was everywhere—radio, television, newspapers. But the situation was even worse than I had imagined. Herbalife had been broadcasting glossy infomercials on a cable channel in Los Angeles. They had used stars like Milton Berle as spokesmen for the Herbalife line of products. Suddenly these programs were canceled. The company was receiving hundreds of calls from worried users of Herbalife products and from distributors unsure of what was going to happen next.

The California attorney general's office, the state Department of Health, and the district attorney of Santa Cruz County also got into the act, accusing Herbalife of making false medical claims for its products and using an illegal pyramid scheme to market them. The Canadian Ministry of Health and Welfare also joined the pack, citing Herbalife for twenty-four violations of Canada's Food and Drug Act. The furor came to the attention of Senator William Roth, chairman of the Senate's permanent subcommittee on investigations. As a result, Herbalife was added to a list of weight-loss products the subcommittee was then looking into. And Rep. John Dingle, chairman of the Subcommittee on Oversight and Investigations of the U.S. House of Representatives, wrote a letter to the Food and Drug Administration (FDA) demanding that the agency hand over copies of its records of its investigation that they claimed had been going on for three years.

I had never heard of any such investigation. I'd been too excited about the product, too busy promoting it, and too focused on building a business. Besides, I was just a country boy. Congressional committees in Washington weren't something I kept tabs on. But I was learning fast about how oppressive big government can be when it puts its mind to it. Talk about a feeding frenzy. You would have thought Herbalife was the Mafia or some other criminal organization! Before the dust had settled, no fewer than five deaths were being linked to the use of Herbalife products.

BIG GOVERNMENT VERSUS HERBALIFE

To my mind, there was little if any connection between these deaths and the product other than the fact that the dead people had been using Herbalife products. But the certainty of the investigators was amazing. To hear them talk, every allegation made, no matter how extreme, had already been proven. The fact was that none of them had been. In my way of thinking, if millions of people had been taking Herbalife and were enjoying healthy lives, why assume that one thing caused the other? It didn't make sense to me.

Mark Hughes, founder of Herbalife, went to Washington to defend the company.

To a bunch of congressmen and medical "experts" bent on putting Herbalife in its place, Mark was in many ways an easy target. Herbalife was based on principles of sound nutrition: a combination of natural herbs, vitamins, and low-fat foods. The company's goal was to provide healthy nutritional products to its customers and a viable business opportunity to its distributors. But Mark's advocacy of those principles rubbed the experts raw. I mean, who was this guy anyway to stand up to medical doctors, government bureaucrats, and the almighty FDA?

In the first place, Mark was just twenty-nine. His parents had divorced when he was a kid, and he had dropped out of school at sixteen. He had been a troubled teen who had used amphetamines and barbiturates and had finally ended up in a residential facility. His mother died of a drug overdose. But somewhere in his young manhood Mark pulled his life together, got interested in nutrition, and realized that he could motivate other people. The media, discovering these facts, made much of them. Those and the fact that, although born poor, Mark had managed to make himself super rich, buy a mansion in Bel Air, and drive luxury cars. When the press wasn't slamming him for his early poverty and lack of education, they were kicking him for having straightened out his life and becoming wealthy.

"Whatever happened to the American dream?" I wondered. The belief you could be born in a slum and, through hard work and perseverance, end up living in a mansion.

So here was Mark on one side of the table and the medical experts of the U.S. government on the other, both sides bumping heads in a major way. To my mind, it was a David vs. Goliath struggle. I followed all these things closely, realizing that my own growing commitment to Herbalife depended on the outcome.

Mark took a lot of flack from the government's witnesses and from the so-called medical experts, who weren't happy to have this upstart from California cut into their territory. It wasn't just the government that had entered the ring with Herbalife. It was also two of the most powerful special-interest groups in America: the American Medical Association and the pillars of the billion-dollar drug industry. Naturally the latter were opposed to Herbalife. They were in the business of selling pills. They and the doctors had a vested interest in a sick America. Not in people making themselves healthy by eating right.

The irony in all the uproar was that none of the accusations against Herbalife was ever proven. After the autopsies and other scientific inquiries, no deaths were attributed to customers having used the product. The much-ballyhooed negative side effects were both mild and predictable since using Herbalife products always required a change in diet. Minor physical discomfort could occur in anyone who introduced new substances into their system.

In the end, the government conceded that no deaths could be attributed to Herbalife. However, they also concluded that it couldn't be proven that Herbalife *hadn't* caused the deaths!

So it was guilt by association. It made Mark Hughes so mad that he filed a multimillion-dollar lawsuit against the FDA for defamation. Mark eventually dropped the suit and accepted an undisclosed settlement rather than subject Herbalife to a long, drawn-out, and very public debate.

HERBALIFE GOES INTO A TAILSPIN

Meanwhile, the financial impact of the investigations was what I had feared. Media attention to the issue had scared a lot of customers away from the product. Distributors just getting started in the business and beginning to reap the financial benefits suddenly found themselves without an income. The company itself was forced to lay off about thirty-two percent of its workforce. My monthly commissions dropped from $100,000 plus to about $7,000. That may not sound that bad until you remember that my current lifestyle required a good deal more than that.

Suddenly the future looked pretty bleak.

But I wasn't ready to go belly-up. I'd spent enough time in that condition in my life and I wasn't going to let it happen again. During the years I had been with Herbalife I had met a whole bunch of people and made a lot of friends. Many were Herbalife distributors in as much a fix as I was. Others were just customers or contacts Barb and I had made around the country in our numerous public appearances. If nothing else, I had learned how to sell an opportunity and a product I believed in. I had learned to be simple and direct with people about what I believed.

About that time Sprint established a subsidiary to sell long-distance phone service using the multilevel marketing plan. The idea was that you'd get a small percentage of the phone bill of each person you signed up. I figured that if selling nutrition products had become risky business in America, I'd use my sales skills to make extra income. So I got together with Jim Fobair, another Herbalife distributor, and we started selling phone service on the side. Within a few weeks, we were the top distributors in the company. We knew a lot of people and, because we had established a reputation for success, a lot of them wanted to get on a bandwagon with our name on it.

Then Mark Hughes found out about our moonlighting. He called us into his office and told us we had to stop.

"What do you mean stop?" I said. "This is keeping us afloat. Besides, this doesn't have anything to do with Herbalife."

"You can't do both," he said flatly. "You're getting everybody off track."

"Off track?" I said. "Everybody is off track already. They're going broke!"

Now you've got to understand that, although Herbalife had been hit hard in America and Canada, its international sales were still going strong and were keeping the company afloat. So while Mark Hughes's personal income had fallen somewhat, he was still a multimillionaire. As for me, I wasn't thinking of just myself. I was thinking of the hundreds of people I'd gotten onto the product and who now were going under. To me, the two businesses—nutrition and economical phone service—complemented each other. If there was a conflict of interest, I just didn't see it.

That wasn't the way Mark saw it, though. He gave us an ultimatum. It was either quit selling phone service or he'd stop our Herbalife checks.

Well, I still believed in Herbalife and didn't want to end my association with the company—much less lose what income came from it. So we followed orders. I put the Sprint business in my daughter's name and Jim put his business in his daughter's name, and the money kept rolling in from the phone business we had already generated.

But then the Sprint operation hit a snag. The company had started charging a ten percent fee for what they called "check processing." This supposedly was to compensate the company for the time and effort to compute what it owed distributors. Call me simple-minded if you want, but it looked like an old-fashioned rip-off to me, a way to increase company profits by cutting into what the company had promised the workers. The dispute ended in a class action lawsuit, and many years later the phone company finally was forced to settle out of court for millions. Shortly after, the Sprint subsidiary itself went under.

These were hard years. I had gotten used to having money, and now doing without it again was more painful than being poor the first time. I sold the 5,000-square-foot house in Palos Verdes, planning to cut costs by buying a less expensive house back in Palm Desert, but ended up getting hit so hard by capital gain taxes that I didn't get far ahead. I still believed that Herbalife would eventually pull out of its nosedive. I just wasn't sure when.

IN OLD MEXICO

Mark Hughes suggested some other distributors and I go to Mexico. He said he'd been thinking of expanding south of the border and there was no time like the present. So in 1988 I took off with a couple of other distributors to Mexico City.

We rented a house in a regular neighborhood. We made contacts and sold product. During the six months we were there, we'd hold meetings every night, and whole families would show up! I didn't speak Spanish, but one of the other guys who did translated for me. Our contacts would have money to spend and be enthusiastic about Herbalife, but we didn't have any product to sell them. I kept calling Mark and asking him when the company was going to open up officially in Mexico. He said soon, but it just didn't happen. We had a lot of business and had to do something.

So we turned into smugglers. We'd drive across the border, load our trunks and suitcases with product we'd buy in El Paso or San Diego, drive back across, and sell the product to our waiting customers. This went on for six months, but it wore us all out. Besides, I missed home. Back there, Barbara hadn't been just sitting around. She was running the business too. It was odd, but when I traveled, we both spent more time on the business.

It was time to look in another direction.

Chapter 11

~

Omnitrition Is Born

ALL MY LIFE I HAD WORKED FOR OTHER people's businesses. Well, except for the few years I was in the carpet cleaning business, and that ended in disaster, although through no fault of my own. But in October 1989, I decided to give working for myself another shot. It happened this way.

Along with my moonlighting for Sprint, I had another gig with a small multilevel marketing operation that sold 3D cameras. The cameras were great, and I sold a bunch of them while I was in Mexico. The income really helped out since my Herbalife checks had fallen off so badly. So when I came back to the States, the guy who ran the company called me and Jim Fobair (another Herbalife distributor who had also been making extra bucks selling cameras) into his office and made us an offer he thought we wouldn't be able to refuse. It seems the company's sales operation was in trouble, and the owner wanted some experienced hands at the helm of the sales force. He knew Jim and I were experienced in multilevel sales and had plenty of contacts. He wanted us to work full-time for the company—to become real executives in the organization.

I admit I was flattered by the offer. I mean, who wouldn't be? The problem was that he didn't want to pay us much for doing the job—a measly one percent of sales.

We knew we were worth more than that, so we said no.

Later that night Jim and I got to talking. I told him I had suddenly realized that we knew a lot more about running a multilevel business than this guy did. In fact, we knew as much, if not more, than just about anybody—about sales, about training, about promotion.

< 67 >

Why, then, were we working for someone else?

Jim Fobair had a friend named Charlie Ragus. Actually, I knew Charlie too but not as well as Jim did. Charlie was originally from Shreveport, Louisiana. He was a big, strapping guy who made a good impression at training sessions. Unlike me or Jim, who had sold mattresses in Minnesota before striking it rich with Herbalife, Charlie had a college education. He had played pro football, had been a top recruiter and Regional Vice President for a major life insurance company, and said he knew how to run a business. Charlie had been in Herbalife too. Like all of us, he had seen his income bottom out to practically nothing.

So the three of us got together to figure out what to do. The first thing we agreed on was that we wanted to stay in multilevel marketing. It was, after all, what we knew best, and among us we had made thousands of contacts over the years with Herbalife. We knew we could depend upon some of those folks who simply couldn't make it the way things were with the company. But we needed a product. Something we could get excited about. We wanted to start simple, with a single product rather than a line. I knew I didn't want to sell another weight-loss program. I was tired of that. But I was still very much into health and nutrition. I might not have been to business or medical school, but during my Herbalife years I had done a lot of reading about nutritional products and felt very educated in the subject. So I said, "What about liquid vitamins? We all need vitamins, and the biggest complaint people have about taking them is having to swallow all those pills and tablets."

Jim and Charlie agreed that it wasn't a bad idea. So, not long after that Charlie was back in Dallas, where he was then living, and ran into the guy who used to make Herbalife's aloe vera drink. Charlie told him about my liquid vitamin idea. He thought it was interesting and said, "Let me work you up some samples."

Not long afterwards, Charlie sent us a jug of this drink. The label said it contained 409 vitamins. It was sweet, fruity, had great color, and was absolutely delicious. Barb and I gulped it down and got really excited. Health drinks we had tried before often tasted like something your mother used to make you take when you were sick. You made a face, held your breath, and hoped your stomach could hold it down. But here was something rich in vitamins that actually tasted terrific!

We served the drink to some of our friends and they were crazy about it too. We decided to call the product OMNI-4. We got the number four from four things the product would do for your body. Later we were advised that name might be interpreted by the FDA as making health claims, so we stopped telling people what the four meant and kept the name anyway. When people asked what it meant, we said: "It means all *for* you."

ON OUR OWN

Our plans were to start the company in January of 1990. Jim and I arranged a conference call with Charlie Ragus to pre-launch the company. We got eighty-eight people on that call! While all we talked about were future plans, they were all so excited they wanted to start right away. "Why not?" I said. The people were there, the enthusiasm was there, the energy was there. I figured there was no time like the present.

We had already decided on a marketing plan for the new company, taking our cues from Herbalife, which despite the legal problems it was then experiencing was a well-run, honest company. We had decided that anybody who signed on as a distributor would have to sell $4,000-worth of product to qualify as a "supervisor," which meant you would earn a percentage of sales of any other distributor you recruited. There was no distributor kit to buy, and no other fees or charges. I wanted people to know that the name of the game was selling product, not just recruiting other distributors.

Well, everybody got really excited about the plan, and we sold $500,000-worth of product our very first month. Our goal had been just $50,000!

And so Omnitrition was born—or at least the idea. We weren't corporate executive types, just good buddies who had learned to admire and trust each other while we were working with Herbalife. We socialized as couples, knew the names of each other's kids, and even loaned each other money to tide us through the desperate times we were experiencing with Herbalife's declining income. Our decision to strike out on our own was based on several concerns. First, a belief that we could take what we had learned from Herbalife and create a company that could provide superior nutritional products with superior benefits to our distributors. Second, a desire to run things ourselves and to run them right.

I could not begin to foresee then what a rough road lay ahead. In the first place, none of us had much money. We were all struggling now to pay bills and keep food on the table. Our venture capital amounted to about $600 we scraped up between us. Someone who really knew how risky start-up businesses were would probably have laughed his head off at our prospects. But we had a dream, enthusiasm, and experience. Besides, Barb was behind the new company every inch of the way. Her confidence really helped to support mine.

BREAKING UP IS HARD TO DO

"Breaking up is hard to do." So says a popular song of a few years back, and one of my first problems was with my former Herbalife associates. When it looked like Omnitrition was going to happen, I called Tish Rochin, who after Barb was my best friend. Tish had been with me in Australia and we had spent literally thousands of hours on the road opening up new areas. I said to her, "Look, Tish, I want to tell you straight because by the time this gets back to you the story will be all twisted a dozen ways. I'm starting my own company but I'm not going to raid or recruit Herbalife distributors."

Tish believed me, I think, but she told her brother Larry and Larry told Mark Hughes. The news didn't please Mark. He decided to stop paying our royalty checks. Our Herbalife income was cut off completely. I was in deep now. It was sink or swim.

Looking back, I can understand why Mark did what he did, although I still think it was wrong. Herbalife was still reeling from the congressional hearings of the 1980s and now a couple of the company's most dependable and productive leaders were going into competition. How else could setting out on our own be interpreted but as a betrayal?

For us, however, it was more survival than betrayal. After all, I thought, Herbalife was a business, not a country or religion. You joined because it provided you with benefits. If the benefits just weren't there anymore, sticking around didn't make a whole lot of sense. Still, in the months after, word spread among the old Herbalife distributors not to speak to us. We were often treated like enemies, and I'm sad to say a lot of the good friends I made in the 1980s weren't speaking to me in the 1990s. It was kind of like leaving Salineville. Around Herbalife headquarters we were Public Enemy Number One.

A DEAL IS STRUCK

We thought about a lawsuit, but then Barb's mom, who had come out to California for a visit, got really sick and we had to put her in a convalescent home. Faced with those expenses, Barb and I got really angry and demanded a meeting with Mark. We were tired of waiting and knew that even if we sued for the money and won, it would take a long time to get it.

We agreed to meet in neutral territory—a hotel lobby near the L.A. airport, not far from Mark's luxurious office at the Herbalife headquarters. Mark wanted to keep our dealings a private matter between him and me. After all, he had done a pretty good job building our image as traitors. I guess he didn't want to be seen negotiating with the enemy.

I remember showing up for the meeting more angry and frustrated than optimistic that the meeting would accomplish anything. Mark could be stubborn when he wanted to be. He hadn't let the FDA or the congressional committees push him around. Why should he pay a couple of ex-distributors who were giving him grief? We didn't have the leverage of the U.S. government to intimidate him.

I think I underestimated the forcefulness of Barb's personality when she knew she was right and was confronting someone she knew wasn't. We no sooner exchanged cool handshakes than Barb put our cards on the table. "Look," she said, "you don't have any right to pull our checks. We didn't do anything wrong, and we *earned* that money honestly."

We had a pretty long talk, and I guess Barb's bluntness paid off. Mark said he'd get back to us. It seems he needed to find a way to pay us without making all his distributors mad.

Mark did get back to us but the check was not in the mail, so to speak. Instead he had a proposition. The deal was this: We could get our money but only if we recruited five new first-line supervisors for Herbalife in a six-month period, achieved a minimum of $5,000 sales volume a month for six months, and had a twenty percent increase in our check.

I couldn't believe what I was hearing. What he was asking for might take an industrious supervisor a year to accomplish, working full-time for Herbalife. And, remember, while this was going on I was busting my behind trying to build a new company. Now I would be forced to work just as hard to collect money I had already earned!

I thought the proposal was ridiculous and told him so. Mark weathered the blast of my outrage and then, without any real defense, explained it would look bad in his own company if he just handed over the money after what we'd done, while if he made us do something to get it then it would seem he had taught us a lesson.

A "lesson!" What kind of lesson? That we were bad people? That we had done something devious or dishonest when the truth was that we had built up one of the largest organizations of distributors in Herbalife—an organization that would stay intact after our departure? For this we should be penalized?

I realized, then, the truth. Our dispute with Mark wasn't about fairness or even money. He knew we had justice on our side, and he had the money to pay us our royalty checks. His reluctance to pay us was all about saving face with his distributors.

Well, I didn't like Mark's conditions, even if they did help him look better to his distributors. I thought they were unfair and illegal since the money withheld from us was money I had already earned. Of course, I wasn't in the position to file a lawsuit that could keep us in court for years and swallow up our benefits in lawyers' fees. Reluctantly, I agreed to the deal.

I don't know whether this surprised Mark or not, but by the end of the first six months we had satisfied all the conditions and more. I say *we*, but it wasn't *us*, it was Barb. She did it herself and, finally, we got the money from Herbalife.

The check, which was over $100,000, really saved our lives—and it paid us enough for Barb's mom to spend her last days in a private convalescent home without the state having to take care of her in one of its facilities. As far as I know, I am the only distributor who ever received an income after he left the company to pursue something else. For the last fifteen years, I have received annually a six-figure income from Herbalife because I follow all the rules and meet all the qualifications every month. Some of the distributors I got involved in Herbalife twenty-three years ago are still there and still doing the business. Only because I got them to believe in the product and I taught them how to build a solid business.

IF ANYTHING CAN GO WRONG, IT WILL

Besides the hassles with Herbalife, development of our new product was also a problem. We had just begun distributing OMNI-4 when it became obvious that our man in Dallas couldn't handle the sheer volume of orders. So we searched for and found another manufacturer. But that's not all we found. Our new manufacturer performed an analysis of OMNI-4 to determine its ingredients and discovered that it didn't contain 409 vitamins at all! In fact, it didn't contain much of anything beyond the vitamins in the fruit juice it was made of.

The product was mostly fruit punch.

No wonder it had tasted so good!

We hadn't been too happy with the product's packaging up to that point either. In the beginning things were pretty basic. The product came in gallon jugs that looked a lot like Clorox bottles. They didn't even come with labels on them! We had to stick the labels (Xerox copies) on with the ingredient description ourselves. They were packaged four bottles to the case. We also had some complaints about the bottles occasionally exploding—a problem we later found out was the result of fermentation of the pineapple juice, one of the ingredients. Even though we had been ripped off by the first guy, I still had faith in the OMNI-4 concept and was determined to get it right.

While flying back from Dallas, I was reading an article about the inventor of the little plastic packets used to squeeze out mustard and ketchup—you know, the packets you get along with your fast-food cheeseburger and fries. The packets were a great idea, solved a pressing problem (who wants jars or bottles in their carry-out bag?), and would be easier to handle. So I started to think, why couldn't OMNI-4 be concentrated and put into plastic packets? The user could add water, we'd lower shipping costs dramatically, and the product would be much more convenient.

But it was only an idea. It was another thing to get an envelope that worked. The plastic envelopes containing thick creamy stuff like mustard and ketchup were one thing. To find packaging that would seal a micellized, watery liquid containing vitamins was another.

We got our manufacturer to begin experimenting, and every time the packaging leaked. You could put it on the counter overnight and it would ooze through the seal. Finally, our manufacturer discovered a process to seal the packages tightly. We also got better-looking labels.

As they say in Houston, "We had liftoff."

Chapter 12

~

New Players, New Problems

WHEN WE STARTED OMNITRITION IN 1989 we were just three guys who had gotten together with a single idea among us and little, if any, cash on hand. Our Herbalife business was disappearing, and our incomes had dropped from the six figures every month to four or less. Jim Fobair and I had been content to let Charlie Ragus run the administrative end of our new business because he said he knew how those things were done. Jim and I were the sales force. We knew how to make contacts, conduct training sessions, and move the product. We trusted Charlie, the college graduate, to run the office, to have the contracts drawn up, and to get Omnitrition on the books as a legitimate corporation. But doing business with Charlie turned out to involve more problems than I had bargained for.

SURPRISES

During the first six months of operation, Charlie had hepatitis and rarely came into the Dallas office, so there was a delay in getting the legal work of incorporating done. Then, when Jim and I flew out to Dallas to finalize the contract, we discovered there weren't just three partners in Omnitrition, but four! An old friend of Charlie's by the name of Thomas Mitchell had been added as a partner and appointed as Chief Administrative Officer and Secretary Treasurer.

I'd never met Thomas Mitchell, who had been a football coach and brought to Omnitrition some valuable business experience, but when

< 75 >

Cover of *OmniNews*, May/June 1991: Roger Daley, Charlie Ragus, and Jim Fobair

I got to know him I liked him. Still, the fact that Charlie hadn't consulted us about Thomas's involvement made me uneasy. Jim and I were given an even bigger shock when we learned how the partnership had been drawn up.

I had thought when we agreed to go into business together that our shares would be equally divided, a third to each man. Instead, the articles of incorporation—drafted by Charlie's lawyer—gave me a twelve percent interest, Jim eighteen percent, Thomas nineteen percent and Charlie fifty-one percent. When we questioned Charlie about this division he explained that the company couldn't be run efficiently unless one partner had controlling interest. He said that since his responsibility was corporate headquarters and its operations it seemed logical that he be fully in charge. Besides, he continued, our income was to be based on the size of our distributor network, not on our partnership shares.

Jim and I considered calling it quits at this point but didn't. Although I didn't find Charlie's reasoning that convincing, I didn't like the alternative either. Jim and I had invested too much time and effort in starting the company to let Charlie's legal sleight-of-hand end our dream.

We signed the contract, and Omnitrition—based until that time on a handshake and a dream—became official.

NETWORKING

Multilevel marketing companies thrive on networking. One contact leads to another, and so it goes. One of our most successful distributors in 1990 was Chris Peterson, who worked out of Minneapolis.

Chris joined Omnitrition in October of 1989, making him among the original distributors. Before joining Omnitrition he hadn't had any experience in person-to-person selling, but Chris put an ad in *USA Today* and it was read by an eight-

Jerry Rubin

een-year-old college student living in upstate New York named Greg Zellars. Greg wanted to make some extra money to meet college expenses and thought Omnitrition might be the key. Trusting in Chris Peterson's example, he placed his own tiny ad in the *New York Times*.

Among the readers of the ad was Jerry Rubin.

You might remember Jerry Rubin from the 1960s. He was the loudest and most obnoxious of protestors among the "Chicago

Seven"—an anti-war, anti-establishment radical group that liked to talk about what was wrong with America and with capitalism in general. If you had asked me whether a guy like Rubin would ever be interested in multilevel marketing, I wouldn't have been able to stop laughing long enough to answer you. From what I remembered, Rubin was interested only in bashing capitalist values.

But Jerry had changed, or so it seemed. Now in his early fifties, he had reinvented himself. He wore a suit, sported a haircut any mother would have approved of, and was into nutrition and jogging. He was still talking about capitalism, but now with a different point to make. Multilevel marketing appealed to him because he thought it was the average man's way of getting rich. Plus, he didn't like the idea of people being forced to work for others. By the spring of 1990, Jerry Rubin was one of Omnitrition's largest independent distributors, with about 400 people in his downline.

THE DURK AND SANDY SHOW

It was Jerry Rubin who hooked Omnitrition up with two of his favorite authors and health gurus—Durk Pearson and Sandy Shaw.

Omnitrition had worked with several scientists to research and develop its product line, but with the arrival of Durk and Sandy product development took a quantum leap forward. Both Durk and Sandy had national reputations and added a lot to the company's credibility. Durk had grown up on a tiny farm, but had ended up graduating from M.I.T., one of the most prestigious universities in the country. He had majored in the subjects I'd avoided in high school—physics, biology, and psychology. As if that wasn't impressive enough, he had triple-minored in chemistry, computer science, and electrical engineering. After graduating, he had become a real rocket scientist at TRW, where he helped develop warheads for the Tomahawk missile.

Sandy Shaw, his collaborator and long-time companion, graduated from UCLA after majoring in both biochemistry and zoology. The two of them were walking encyclopedias, and by the time I was introduced to them they were nationally renowned nutritional scientists. Their

Sandy Shaw and Durk Pearson

book, *Life Extension: A Practical Scientific Approach*, had become a nationwide best-seller. They had appeared on hundreds of TV talk shows and science specials, and had done over a thousand radio broadcasts.

Durk and Sandy had developed a special type of water-and fat-soluble vitamin C. And it was Durk who solved the problem of the fermenting pineapple juice that had plagued OMNI-4. With the help of Durk and Sandy we began to expand our product line beyond the basic OMNI-4, and they brought us their line of "Designer Foods." These consisted of WOW, a caffeinated coffee substitute, GO FOR IT (a de-caf version of WOW), and FOCUS (food for the brain). They also introduced us to the world of herbs, expanding our understanding of how natural ingredients used for centuries in Asia and elsewhere could be beneficial if made available to the increasingly health-conscious American public.

What can I say about Durk and Sandy? Well, for one thing, although clearly brilliant, they looked more like 1960s hippies than conventional science types. Durk was tall and lean as a rake. He had blond, unkempt, shoulder-length hair and wore shorts and muscle shirts that revealed almost no body fat. Sandy was short and dark-haired. She liked to bend iron horseshoes to show off the physical strength she had gotten from the nutritional formulations she and Durk had designed. As spokespersons for the company, they were a dynamic duo. They were entertaining and had a natural gift for making complicated scientific stuff seem clear as a bell to ordinary people like me. I don't think anyone who ever met these two forgot the experience. They were brilliant, and they were outrageously different. I can't deny that during their association with the company both benefited from the association, even though the relationship would sour later in the story.

In the meantime, during that first year of operation, there were other disturbing signs of things to come. Charlie had set up company headquarters in Dallas in a little rinky-dink office across from a trucker hotel. As president, he ran the company from that end while Jim lived in Minnesota and I lived in California and worked to get distributorships established. In those early days, my official title was Vice President and National Marketing Director, but basically we viewed ourselves as distributors too. That was to be the Omnitrition tag line: A company built by distributors for distributors. Maybe it was our fault that things happened the way they did. Maybe we should have realized that a handshake wasn't enough for security when big money is at stake.

Meanwhile, I was working my butt off. In February of 1991, for example, I did "business opportunity meetings" in Detroit, Fort Lauderdale, Denver, New York City, and all over California. They weren't the four corners of the earth, but they were the four corners of the country. We moved from our tiny original office to more spacious facilities in Carrollton, a Dallas suburb. Maybe the biggest sign of success was our fledgling company's income—$12 million in sales the first year!

ONE PARTNER LESS

It wasn't too long before we were having trouble getting our share of the profits. We hadn't been paid for four months and things at home were getting pretty tight. We were also hearing disturbing rumors about the way Charlie Ragus was handling things at the home office. So Jim and I went to Dallas for a meeting. After a long negotiation, Charlie agreed to our demand for twenty-five percent for each partner. But later Charlie fired Thomas Mitchell and ended up with Thomas's shares, and fifty-one percent!

It was clear who was in charge, and Jim and I didn't like it.

This time when we objected, Charlie told us if we didn't like the way he was running things we could just buy him out.

This took my breath away. I didn't have any money to do that and I knew Jim didn't either, and we told Charlie so. "No problem," he said, "you can buy me out in installments. We can stretch payments out over five years, then everybody will be happy."

Time payments. The great American way.

We agreed. Both Jim and I knew our relationship with Charlie was at an end. The trust just wasn't there anymore. Besides, Charlie had been running the office, shuffling papers, and dealing with lawyers. The real engine powering the company was the sales force—Jim and I. I figured we could always hire a good office manager. That person didn't need to be a partner with a big draw on company profits.

So in 1991 Jim and I agreed to buy out Charlie Ragus's share of the company. By the way, it didn't take five years to pay off Charlie. We did it in two years! Things really took off after that. Then we hit a major snag, and it just about sank the whole ship.

Top: Omnitrition Jet, Roger and
Barbara Daley

Left: Roger Daley

Chapter 13

~

The Webster Suit

CHARLIE RAGUS HAD AGREED to sell his share of the company for $2.5 million. We hired the Dallas law firm of Gardere & Wynne, one of the largest firms in Texas, to represent us in the purchase. Jim Fobair and I were off and running as fifty-fifty partners. We increased our product line to fifteen products, and we had over 50,000 distributors. Omnitrition had come a long way in just a little over two years. We were frequently touted as the class act of the MLM industry.

THE WEBSTER SUIT: ROUND ONE

In 1992 Shawn Webster, Robert Ligon, and four other distributors from California and Texas filed a class action lawsuit against Omnitrition claiming the company was a pyramid scheme, making money not on retail sales but on the recruitment of new distributors. Although this allegation was false and outrageous, the very fact that it went to court caused the company and me a lot of grief. The plaintiffs in the case had offered to settle out of court, but I said no, despite the high legal costs we were piling up. I wanted nothing on any public record to suggest that we were buying people off. That would be like admitting the allegations were true. I had worked too long and too hard to achieve integrity within the industry to give in to legal blackmail.

Omnitrition's marketing plan at the time the suit was filed was basically this: A person joined Omnitrition by application. Upon approval, the applicants became known as Independent Marketing

< 83 >

Associates (IMAs). These were the distributors—the ground-level sellers of our products. IMAs could buy products from Omnitrition at a twenty percent discount and resell them to the general public, but no IMA was ever under any obligation to sell or to purchase products. An IMA could then become a supervisor. Bronze supervisors—the lowest-level supervisor—could qualify by selling $4,000 in one month or $2,000 in two consecutive months. The supervisor was entitled to a forty percent discount, plus a sliding-scale wholesale profit based upon future purchases of his or her downline (i.e., IMAs recruited by the distributor and part of his or her network), and a four percent royalty "override" on sales of three generations of qualified supervisors. All supervisors, regardless of level, had to certify that they had made ten retail sales to ten customers per month in order to receive royalties.

It may sound complicated, but the plan was designed to encourage and reward initiative and guarantee that Omnitrition was in the business of selling health products, not just recruiting distributors. In other words, no one got paid unless products were sold! This was a good system. I believed it complied with the law, and I was determined to defend it against these false charges.

The case was heard by Judge Saundra Brown Armstrong of the United States District Court. Judge Armstrong rendered summary judgment in our favor on July 25, 1994. Basically what the court said was that, considering the criteria for pyramid schemes established by earlier court decisions (standards agreed upon by all parties in the case!), Omnitrition was *not* a pyramid scheme. It also found that no supervisor or distributor in our system could earn rewards unrelated to actual product sales merely for recruiting other participants.

To put it even more simply, what Judge Armstrong said was this: the complainers couldn't prove their case. They couldn't prove that Omnitrition was more interested in headhunting than product sales, or that Omnitrition's enforcement policies were inadequate. They couldn't even prove that any of the plaintiffs had ever lost money working as distributors for the company. Shawn Webster, the ringleader among the plaintiffs, admitted under oath that he sold or personally consumed all of the products he purchased and as a result either made a profit or at least broke even.

If the Webster suit had ended there—as I thought it had—Omnitrition might have been one of the very few MLM companies officially declared by a U.S. Federal Court not to be a pyramid scheme. As it turned out, we weren't going to get off that easy, despite Judge Armstrong's determination that we had won hands down as a matter of law. Webster and company appealed the verdict to the Ninth Circuit Court of Appeals and there, on a different day, with a different judge, the case was sent back to be tried.

ROUND TWO

We had won the first round of the Webster suit on the basis of a summary judgment, which basically meant that Webster's case just didn't hold up on the face of the facts agreed upon by both parties. But on appeal, Webster's lawyers argued that there were material facts that a trial court should have determined and that therefore a summary judgment wasn't appropriate. The case was submitted on September 12, 1995, and decided on March 4, 1996. Omnitrition lost this round.

We lost not because the court said Omnitrition was a pyramid scheme, but because it decided that a trial was needed to prove that it *wasn't*. So we were left with the opinion of one Ninth-Circuit judge that Omnitrition wasn't a pyramid scheme and the opinion of another court—and unfortunately, a higher one—that the issue remained unsettled.

The Appeals Court decision was like a kick in the gut to me. It seemed fundamentally unfair. Call me naive but I always thought that in America you were innocent until you were proven guilty. The Appeals Court had seemed to assume the opposite, shifting the burden to Omnitrition to prove we *weren't* guilty. Not only that, but the "grieved parties" in the case hadn't even been able to show that they had lost any money with the company. So what was this case all about anyway?

By this time I was pretty disillusioned by the court system, but why should I have been surprised? I had seen what governmental agencies could do during the ephedra episode. At the same time we were stuck with another problem. Our legal fees in defending the suit had cost the company millions of dollars. In this great country of ours, whether you win or lose, the lawyers always win.

Now I had a decision to make. I could continue fighting the suit and run up even more legal bills, or I could negotiate for some sort of settlement. As it turned out, Shawn Webster and his confederates were equally weary of big legal bills. Besides, they knew very well they could not be sure of winning if the case were to go to trial. Although we had lost the advantage of a summary judgment, they were still far from winning if their class action suit actually proceeded to trial. Besides, the case had already taken up four years. How many more years would pass before the case was resolved—six, eight, ten? I was finding out the hard way that the wheels of justice turn, but they turn slowly—and sometimes they don't just turn, they grind.

ROUND THREE

So the Webster case ended the way most lawsuits end—with one set of lawyers talking to another set of lawyers and everybody agreeing to pick up their marbles and go home. Only the lawyers went home richer, and the parties involved went home poorer but wiser. Since neither Webster nor Ligon could ever prove they lost money with Omnitrition, I guess the money we shelled out to get them to drop the suit was all gravy for them. You could call it a payoff if you want, but at that point I didn't feel I could continue to drain company resources with lawyers' fees.

It wasn't just the fees. It was the negative energy, the constant aggravation. I hated depositions and so-called experts and the wrangling atmosphere of the courtroom. I hated testifying and being grilled by lawyers. I had a business to run, a family to care for, a life to live. Settling the Webster suit was a bitter pill for Barb and me to swallow, but we did.

It was time to move on.

Chapter 14

~

The Mexican Connection

CREATED A LOT OF BUSINESS and business opportunities for Herbalife back in the 1980s. Yet in many ways it was a frustrating experience. Mexico had some pretty strict laws about what foreign companies could and could not do, and while I was there Herbalife never succeeded in opening a distribution center in Mexico. I had to buy product in Texas or California and haul it across the border in a suitcase. As I said earlier, sometimes I felt more like a smuggler than a salesman.

Despite those problems, I had seen firsthand the wonderful opportunities awaiting a company eager to do business in Mexico. Most Mexicans had grown up with home remedies and products based on simple, natural substances that offered them the hope of staying healthy. Basically, when you're poor, you can't afford to get sick. It's cheaper to eat healthy. So in 1991 we decided to expand our Omnitrition business into Mexico by creating a subsidiary corporation called Omnitricion de Mexico, or Omni-Mex as we called it around the office.

Omni-Mex was Charlie Ragus's baby because, at that time, he was still majority shareholder in the company. But the guy who was in charge as president of Omni-Mex was to be a Mexican national named Jorge Vergara Madrigal.

< 87 >

MY FRIEND JORGE

I had met Jorge in my Herbalife days. He had dark, curly hair and a bushy mustache, and he would eventually play a bigger and more troublesome role in my life than I supposed at the time.

Before I met him, Jorge had been a little bit like me. He'd knocked around from job to job. He'd been an office boy, and a maitre d' in a restaurant. He'd sold cars and real estate and made a pile of money. He even started a company to sell pork to roadside taco stands. But then through some accounting screwup he began losing money and finally ran up over a million pesos in debt. Easy come, easy go.

But Jorge's real problem wasn't his bank account. It was his health. He had astronomically high cholesterol and a lot of stress in his life, which made him a likely candidate for an early checkout. Then, while he still lived in Mexico, he found Herbalife and enrolled as a distributor. It wasn't that he had a lot of faith in multilevel marketing, he told me later. He was just desperate to survive.

Jorge started using the products, got his cholesterol under control, and then came to the United States, where he learned the business. In those days Jorge was down on his luck. He didn't even own a car. But he learned fast and in a short time became a super salesman with a strong testimonial as to how Herbalife had allowed him to become stronger and healthier. He returned to Mexico.

When I went down to Mexico to sell Herbalife products I depended on Jorge a lot and we got to be friends. After all, I couldn't speak Spanish, so he pretty much ran things. He loved to eat, and he knew where all the great restaurants were. He laughed a lot and had a gift for gab—in Spanish or English. We traveled all over Mexico selling Herbalife products and recruiting distributors.

Although Jorge and I worked together and had friendly relations, he wasn't so popular with everyone in the company. The truth was that to some people in the home office, to whom Mexicans were automatically second-class citizens, Jorge was just a "dumb Mexican." They'd make jokes behind his back, poke fun at his accent, and question whether he was up to running the Mexican operation.

Jorge Vergara (Mexico partner) and Roger Daley

These weren't attitudes that create a lot of mutual trust, but rather the kind that invite getting even. And they explain a lot of what happened later.

Anyway, in the late 1980s when Herbalife was getting dumped on by regulatory agencies and lawsuits, Jorge stayed with Herbalife. The ride wasn't as rough in Mexico, where the government was friendlier to a successful business enterprise, but in 1991 Jorge decided to leave Herbalife. He became our point man in opening Mexico to Omnitrition.

THE SHELL GAME

Ever heard of the shell game? It's a common magician's trick. The magician moves a little ball around on a table in front of the audience and puts it underneath one of three shells. Then he switches the positions of the shells and you've got to choose which shell contains the ball.

If the magician's really good, you'll pick the wrong shell, no matter how carefully you've watched the magician's hands. You see, the guy's hands are quicker than your eyes. Besides, there's always a trick to it and you don't know what it is.

Jorge Vergara, Charlie
Ragus: Salude of Mexico
City

Jorge Vergara and Roger
Daley: grand opening,
Guadalajara, Mexico

That's the way it was in Mexico with our Omnitricion de Mexico adventure. A shell game we ultimately lost.

Omni-Mex was incorporated as our Mexican subsidiary in May of 1991, while Charlie Ragus was still Omnitrition's majority partner. In the beginning, we were excited and optimistic about the Mexican expansion. Charlie was big on the Mexican investment. He knew Jorge and, while he didn't like him very much, he knew he was the kind of guy who could get Omni-Mex off to a terrific start.

We thought we had good legal support too in Doug Adkins, our corporate counsel. We had hired Doug earlier to handle the purchase of Charlie's Omnitrition stock. Adkins was partner in Gardere & Wynne. And talk about connections! He was a director of the Fellowship of Christian Athletes, an active Deacon of the First Baptist Church of Dallas, counsel to the Dallas Mavericks in the NBA, and one of the founders of an organization that assists residents in Mexico with free medical and dental services. This guy was so righteous and religious he used to open our conferences with him with prayer!

With a guy like that, what's not to trust?

Lots, we found out later.

When we planned our Mexican subsidiary, we wanted to ensure we had a controlling (eighty percent) interest in the company. But according to Mexican law, a foreign corporation could not have a majority interest in a company without the approval of the Mexican government. Doug assured us that his firm had an office in Mexico. He said that a Gardere & Wynne lawyer named Charlie Meachum could shepherd our application through the Mexican Foreign Investment Commission, the approving agency.

But later I learned that G&W's so-called Mexican office was hardly more than a letter drop. What really happened was that Adkins subcontracted with a Mexican law firm to act as local counsel in Mexico. Then Adkins dealt directly with the Mexican firm without keeping us apprised of what was going on. And what was going on was a long and complicated story.

As an interim structuring of the company, ownership was issued in shares. According to the initial division, Omnitrition owned forty-nine percent, Jorge Vergara owned ten percent, and the remainder was held in trust by other Mexican nationals with the understanding that when the Mexican government had approved Omnitrition's majority ownership, these shares would be transferred back to us. These "straw shareholders" were Rubin Ruiz—Jorge's brother-in-law—Carlos Perez, and Eduardo Sanchez.

But by December of 1991, the Mexican "ownership" of Omni-Mex became more complicated. Carlos Perez and Jorge had a falling out when Jorge accused Perez of diverting Omni-Mex funds for his own personal use. Perez denied the charge, but agreed to let Jorge buy his shares. At the same time Eduardo Suarez, an original shareholder, transferred his two shares to Alberto Lopez, another Mexican national. If you're confused at this point, as I often was, the bottom line was that Jorge Vergara and his wife together ended up with nineteen percent of the company, and Jorge became President. I was appointed Vice President.

But that was only part of the story. After Jim Fobair and I bought out Charlie's interest in the company in February of 1992, Jorge and Omnitrition signed a Letter of Agreement whereby Jorge would receive an additional twenty-nine shares (for a total of forty-nine percent) if he would comply with a set of conditions. From the time Omni-Mex had started, we had communication and accountability problems with Jorge's operations. Sometimes it seemed almost a nightmare of conflicting information and reports, squabbles over shipments, boardroom politics, and accounting irregularities. Money due some American distributors had not been paid, and Jorge had made some administrative changes not approved by the Board. We hoped this offer of nearly a half interest would encourage Jorge to comply with the Board's decisions and correct reporting irregularities.

That's basically where we stood while we waited for the Mexican Foreign Investment Agency to okay our majority control.

THE PLOT THICKENS

There wasn't anything illegal or dishonest about any of these strategies. Other companies trying to get started in Mexico had done the same thing. They used Mexican nationals as "friendly shareholders," and when the government approved, the shares were surrendered to their intended owners. The plan wasn't flawed. The people involved were. Anyone with common sense might have seen the trouble brewing, but we got blindsided by our own lawyers as well as by our old *amigo*, Jorge.

What happened after that even I never completely understood, and certainly didn't understand at the time it was all going down. After all, you pay lawyers big bucks to negotiate and oversee transactions, don't you? When we went to court later against Gardere & Wynne for screwing up the deal, our new lawyers had to use a chalkboard and diagrams to explain to the jury what had happened.

So as best I can tell it—without a chalkboard or diagrams—the whole plot went like this:

On June 18, 1992, we received approval for the "demexicaniza-tion" of Omni-Mex and the acquisition of enough shares from our straw shareholders to bring Omnitrition's ownership to eighty percent. A week later the Omni-Mex shareholders met and authorized the stock transfer as we originally planned, calling upon Jorge's wife, Mr. Perez, and Mr. Lopez Arguado to transfer their shares to Omnitrition International. Score: Omnitrition eighty percent, Jorge twenty percent.

At least that was the plan.

But that's when the trouble started. Jorge, as it turned out, had his own ideas about how the shares should be divided and it didn't square with our plan. He argued that, according to the Letter of Agreement, he was to have fifty percent of Omni-Mex. That couldn't be true, because it was always Jim's and my intention to retain control of the company. That is, with at least fifty-one percent. When our attorney told Jorge he wasn't authorized to divide shares as he had intended, he told him to "take a hike," and refused to sign the minutes of the meeting, which would have made the Board's decision legal and authorized the transfer of the shares. Instead, he had his secretary substitute his own revised instruction authorizing the transfer of one of his wife's two shares, and the Perez and Suarez shares—to himself! These transfers were made without his fulfilling the conditions of the Letter of Agreement.

His justification at the time was that by transferring all these shares to him we could avoid paying additional taxes. This, he argued, was both simpler and more economical. "Why pay taxes you could avoid?" he reasoned. Jorge probably also thought he deserved half ownership in the company anyway, just as Jim Fobair had promised.

About the same time, Jorge dismissed the Mexican firm that had been handling Omni-Mex's legal affairs and hired the firm of new attorney, Eric Coufal. Jorge requested all files regarding Omni-Mex be sent to his new attorney. This transfer was authorized, but what our lawyers didn't realize was that the files included unsigned share certificates held in the name of Perez and Lopez. Jorge transferred these to himself. Jorge and his wife had succeeded in bringing fifty-one percent under their control!

"IT'S JUST BUSINESS, ROGER"

Looking back at this, I can only say that Adkins and the Mexican lawyer should have foreseen the risk in letting the stock certificates slip into Jorge's hands. They should have let Jim and me know (we were still partners then) what dangers lay in Jorge's maneuvers. But when the deal was done, it was too late for regrets. The whole idea of "friendly shareholders" is that you can trust them to surrender the shares when the time comes. But when the time came, Jorge said "no," which means the same thing in Spanish and English.

As I said before, Jorge had his reasons. He had not always gotten a square deal from my associates. As I have said, some of them dismissed him as a "dumb Mexican," a screwup who couldn't get reports in on time and who owed money to the home office and wouldn't pay up. Our relations with Jorge had been rough sledding ever since Omni-Mex started. Charlie, and later Jim Fobair, had been constantly critical of the Mexican operation. For Jorge, grabbing up the share certificates was like finding money in the street. Finders keepers, losers weepers.

It was, as Jorge later explained to me, "Just business, Roger. Nothing personal. Just business."

I suspect Jorge thought that after all the under-table dealings we could be friends—laugh off the hurt and go out and get enchiladas and tacos like in the old days. But the reality was that Jorge had obtained a controlling interest in Omni-Mex, and Omnitrition was eventually forced out of Mexico altogether.

Jorge's fancy footwork with Omnitrition shares wasn't the end of the Mexican story. Later, in 1993, Jorge was suing Omnitrition International, charging that Omni-Mex had loaned money to Jim, Barbara, and me. It simply wasn't true. For our part, we had to take Jorge to court because he had tried to make a separate deal to obtain his product from Life Services, Inc., our supplier, in direct breach of Omni-Mex's exclusive supply agreement with us.

Then, in June of that year we learned that Jorge had called a meeting of Omni-Mex distributors in Guadalajara. There he announced that Omni-Mex was no longer in business and that he was forming a new corporation called Omnilife. Omnilife, he said, would be 100 percent Mexican-owned.

A FINAL IRONY

In 1999 the prestigious *Wall Street Journal* featured a long, front-page article on Jorge and his achievements. It was written in such superlatives that you might have thought it was prepared by Jorge's own public relations department. It presented Jorge in heroic light as a brilliant, charismatic entrepreneur who had built Omnilife from the ground up and all along the way had trumped all his competitors, including his old company Herbalife.

These days Jorge is riding high. The largest of his units, Omnitricion de Mexico, showed sales after discounts and commissions of $106 million in the eleven months through November 1998. He has big plans to build a $270 million cultural complex in Guadalajara.

Accompanying the article is a headshot of Jorge. He still sports that bushy mustache that was his trademark, but these days he appears more jowly, portly, and self-satisfied than I remember him.

Given the profits he has made that should have been shared with me and other Omnitrition investors, I'm not surprised. The article makes no mention of his fancy footwork with the Omnitrition shares. My son-in-law spoke to the *Journal* reporter and offered them another view of Jorge and their story. The editor promised to check it out.

I'm still waiting. In fact, a couple of years later they printed the same story again. Your truthful *Wall Street Journal*.

Chapter 15

∼

Conspiracies

THE WEBSTER SUIT AND THE MEXICAN RIP-OFF were stress-ful for the company and for me, but as it turned out there were even more bumps and potholes in the road ahead. Webster and the others had been disgruntled Omnitrition supervisors with their own axes to grind. But by the time they had filed suit in 1992, they had left the company. So in a way I looked at their attack as an attack by outsiders. It was *them* against us. As a company, we stood strong against the attack.

What's worse is when the attack comes from within, and that's how things were shaping up in most of 1992 and 1993. Jim Fobair (my remaining partner) and I had known each other from the Herbalife days, and even though our personalities were different and we occa-sionally disagreed on management decisions, I considered him a close friend as well as a business partner.

But from our joint acquisition of the company, our relationship had begun to show signs of stress. In the first place, sharing power with Jim wasn't that easy. We had different visions, different manage-ment styles, sometimes different goals, and usually different means of achieving them. I wanted Omnitrition to be not only the most success-ful multilevel marketing company in the country, but the most ethical too. I think sometimes Jim got impatient with my concern that the company have a zero-tolerance policy on violations of compliance pro-cedures.

Besides these issues, there were personal ones. Jim was married with children, but he had found a new love interest, a woman named Rosie. Rosie was a flashy blonde who claimed—falsely, we later dis-

< 97 >

covered—to have been a former Miss Chile. Jim didn't do a whole heck of a lot to hide the affair. He and Rosie would travel together, show up at parties and even company meetings. Completely wowed by her, he bought her expensive presents and wined and dined her, often on the company tab. Finally, he managed to find her a place at the company office, largely I suspected because she convinced him that since he rarely went into the office he needed a spy to look after his interests.

Rosie was a troublemaker and a gossip, and in a short time she had managed to make herself a force to be reckoned with in the company even though she had no official position and most of us, particularly our employees, found her pushy and obnoxious. While in Mexico, she made herself such a burr under Jorge's saddle that he wrote a memo to Jim complaining about her lies and gossip and insisting that she stay out of the country.

Barb and I felt sorry for Jim's wife, whom we considered to be a good friend. She was completely blindsided by Jim's affair. But our efforts to warn Jim against Rosie's negative influence on him and on the company didn't do much for our friendship or business relationship. Jim didn't want to listen. He was in love—or at least heavily in lust.

As a result of this conflict and other disagreements, the company seemed to be dividing into two warring camps—with Jim having his supporters and I having mine.

It wasn't just Jim. Jerry Rubin had become a powerful influence on a lot of distributors, who were impressed by his reputation as former anti-establishment figurehead and his easy access to the national media. While I commended the way Jerry had reinvented himself and how he was now supporting the system rather than undermining it, I had begun to realize that he had his own agenda within the company. I knew that his alliance with Jim Fobair was going to work to my disadvantage.

THE RUMOR MILL

During that time I became aware of nasty rumors circulating among the distributors—and in the home office—about me, about Barb, and about my management of the company. The innuendoes and gossip were not only false, they were just plain slanderous. It was rumored that I had embezzled $15,000 from the company to take my family—and pets!—on vacation. Another rumor was that I had created cushy jobs for my son, and signed a long-term lease on a corporate jet just so my son-in-law could fly it! It was further reported that I had fired key office personnel without cause. We had in those days—and have still—a voice mail system where we could send messages to every IMA in the company instantaneously. These "global messages," as we called them, generally were used to announce upcoming meetings, conduct trainings, and report good news about company sales or promotions.

Suddenly, I discovered the global message system was being used to spread rumors and accusations about me. In addition, I learned secret meetings were held and alliances were being formed at business opportunity meetings. Word was spreading that Jim was going to buy me out and I was going to retire to the desert and play golf. Some distributors were urged to send faxes to me directly demanding that I step down. Others were told not to order new product so that the company would grind to a halt. What began as a company unified behind a great vision had become a hotbed of dissension, mistrust, and conspiracy-mongering.

Most of these rumors were invented; some had a basis in fact but were twisted or exaggerated to serve Jim Fobair's takeover plans. Of these, the "Mafia connection" was probably the most bizarre. In October of 1993 we had hired a man from New York as a business consultant. He was the father of one of our top distributors and a man whom we were told had had a lot of experience in city government. He was of Italian descent, as are a great many Americans. As he became highly visible in the company, his ancestry seemed to trigger the ethnic prejudices—and fantasies—of some of Jim Fobair's followers. Later, I heard there were meetings in which Jim would make thinly veiled references to "certain persons whose names ended in vowels" and create fears that big-time, organized crime was about to swallow the company.

It all made a great story, but that's all it was. Ten months after the man in question joined the company, I decided that the business reputation that preceded him was over-inflated and he was more interested in feathering his own nest ($10,000 per week salary!) than helping Omnitrition get to the next level. He resigned at my request.

In the case of another rumor, I must plead half-guilty. I did fire two prominent home office employees, and had them escorted from the building by the Dallas police. These were Joy Allen and Steve Jamieson. Joy was a former Herbalife office worker I had known in California; Steve was her much-younger live-in boyfriend. When they first came to work for Omnitrition as public relations consultants, Steve represented himself as a former professional baseball player and talent scout for a big Hollywood agency. (Later, we found out that although he had held some kind of job with a talent agency, the professional baseball story was invented.) Steve was supposed to have had a lot of connections, and claimed to be able to do great things to publicize the company. But Steve was more talk than action, and he stirred up a lot of trouble.

At first, Steve and Joy seemed to play both sides of the fence, so to speak, in order to feel out which partner would be more vulnerable to their influence. They began a divide-and-conquer strategy, and eventually aligned themselves with Jim Fobair, who was easier for them to manipulate. Once they had Jim in their pocket, they began to tape private conversations, spread malicious rumors, and contribute to an atmosphere of negativity, suspicion, and discontent around the home office.

When I had had enough, I gave them their walking papers. End of story. Or so I thought!

KANGAROO COURT

In October, things came to a head. Behind my back, Jim and Jerry Rubin had contacted about seventy distributors from all over the country and persuaded them to come to Dallas for a secret meeting by frightening them with dire warnings that, unless I was dumped, the company would go under and they would lose their five-figure income. They met in a Dallas hotel and worked out a list of questions I was to be asked—questions that were to be answered with a simple "yes" or "no" and guaranteed to make me appear incapable of running the company and look like a crook.

I wasn't aware of any of this plotting at the time and showed up the next morning for work as usual. All of a sudden I saw a huge charter bus pull up to our building. The door opened and dozens of our distributors got out and came marching through our front door. Even Jim Fobair came in, which was unusual since he liked to avoid the office as much as possible. Jim explained that the distributors had arrived to express some of their concerns about the way I was running the company. "Fine," I said, still a little uncertain as to why the "concerns" couldn't be handled by simple phone calls. We all went down to the break room, which was a large space we sometimes used for company meetings.

All the major players in the conspiracy had shown up, including Jerry Rubin, Jim Fobair and his girlfriend Rosie, Bill Elsberg, who at that time was one of Jim's closest allies and the man who ran the meeting, and Bill's wife, Sandy.

Although the confrontation was a surprise attack, it didn't take me long to figure out which way the wind was blowing and what was at stake. This wasn't a company meeting. It was a carefully orchestrated lynching.

The meeting no sooner got underway than Bill Elsberg started firing questions at me. Had I charged certain expenses to the company? Had I had Rosie investigated? As the conspirators planned, I wasn't allowed to explain any answers, only to respond "yes" or "no."

It was clear from the beginning that Bill Elsberg was looking for incriminating answers because he wouldn't let me explain anything. Yes, I had taken the family dogs on a plane trip at company expense, but I wasn't allowed to explain that I had reimbursed the company for the alleged "criminal act." I hadn't had Rosie investigated, but Doug Adkins, our corporate attorney, had—on his own and for good reason. The investigation exposed her for the manipulator she was and had saved the company a world of future grief.

Jim Fobair had not allowed any of the office staff into the meeting, even though it was held during lunch hour and at a time when they normally would have been using the break room. But I found out later that a lot of them listened at the door. It was clear that he and his allies didn't want any of the charges against me contradicted by the office staff, most of whom respected me as the company's leader. Some of the distributors spoke up on my behalf too. This infuriated Jim's faction.

But although bad news for me, the meeting didn't quite turn out the way the conspirators had expected. For one thing, after a loud debate that got louder and more tense as the meeting went on, some of the distributors stayed loyal to me, and when many started protesting some of the more outrageous accusations, Jerry Rubin, an expert in public confrontation, started yelling back.

So as a lynching, the conspiracy collapsed because they failed to stay unified. Yet the warring camps were still in place, and after the meeting some of the distributors participated in a nationwide conference call that any Omnitrition distributor could listen to and compressed the events of several hours into a five-minute version of my answers.

Of course, they presented me in the worst possible light.

AFTERMATH

Over the years, I have relived that day many times. I imagine how I might have answered differently, and I experience again the pain of betrayal by business associates, many of whom I had once counted as friends. I had been in real courts of law where I had to defend the company and myself, but never in so excruciating a situation as this kangaroo court.

It was clear what the conspirators wanted—a hostile takeover of the company. But it was also clear to me that that was going to happen over my dead body.

CIVIL WAR

After that, being around the office was no picnic. I tried to stay away and stay focused on the business. But the personal attacks, false accusations, and divisive tactics of Fobair and his cohorts continued and even got worse. The company's voice mail system became a major tool to spread the lies. The company had become a war zone. I got so concerned, I had an electronic sweep conducted in my house and office because I thought the phone lines might have been tapped. That's what the atmosphere was like around the Omnitrition home office at the end of 1993.

There was nothing to do but take Fobair and the other conspirators to court. The company retained the law firm of Graham, Bright & Smith to represent it against Jim and the conspiring distributors. The court appointed a "Special Master" who would run day-to-day operations until the issues in the case were resolved. His name was Bonner Geddes. Bonner was a good man, who ran things evenhandedly. Ironically, after the court relieved him of his duties, Bonner became an Omnitrition distributor.

DEALING WITH THE DEVIL

During this time it became clear to me that there was only one way Omnitrition could survive—one partner would have to buy the other out. Jim was of the same mind.

In November and December of 1993, discussions got underway as to just how that could be accomplished. Since I had worked with Jim before on contractual agreements I knew he could drive a hard bargain. What made it worse was the atmosphere of mistrust and dislike that had resulted from the vicious spread of malicious rumors and from the kangaroo court. By the first of the new year, I had reached a tentative agreement whereby Jim would sell his shares back to me for $500,000. But then he boosted his price to $750,000 in anticipation of profits from sales of Omnitrition products to Mexico.

Jim also wanted certain concessions that would allow him to start his own competing MLM company. This was a sticking point in negotiations between us.

On January 6, Jim and I went to the office of one of our attorneys to meet with Jorge Vergara and other representatives of Omni-Mex. The meeting was productive—or so it seemed. We all agreed that it was better to do business together than to litigate. It was clear to me that all efforts to resolve our differences were futile and the only viable solution was a complete break.

As a part of the buyout, Jim and I agreed to split Omnitrition's net profits from the sale of goods to Mexico fifty-fifty. Jim was to promise not to compete with Omni-Mex in Mexico with his new company, should he form one. It looked like things were pretty wrapped up and that the end of conflict within the company was in sight. Boy was I wrong. Little did I know that Fobair had already formed a company and was ready to go into business the day after we finalized our agreement.

Even as we sat at the table, we were laying the groundwork for another lawsuit without even realizing it.

Chapter 16

~

Life in a War Zone

JANUARY 13, 1994, was a big day for me. For the first time since starting Omnitrition in 1989, I was going it alone. I was the sole owner of Omnitrition and its subsidiaries, and I was optimistic, believing that the change would clear away major obstacles and leave the company in position for tremendous growth. Our accountants had projected our revenue for the upcoming year to be $62 million with a profit of $8.4 million. But before the company could grow, we had to recover from the divisive events that preceded the buyout.

In the first place, Omnitrition had been fractured. Jim Fobair, my now ex-partner, had taken many distributors and a few of the office staff (including Steve and Joy) with him to start his new company. In the second place, my troubles with Jim weren't finished. There were still some issues to resolve connected with my purchase agreement and a lot of hard feelings on both sides. A person just looking at the company from the outside might have thought the war was over, but I had the uneasy feeling we were still operating in a war zone with the distinct possibility there might be more casualties.

MEXICO AGAIN

When Jim Fobair and I were ending our unhappy relationship, the Mexican issue came up again. After Jorge pulled his "stock" stunt, we refused to pay him his percentages from Omnitrition sales in Mexico. He sued, claiming Omnitrition International owed him money. When Fobair and I were negotiating, we agreed with Jorge to settle the suit.

< 105 >

The deal we made was that we would not compete with Omni-Mex in Mexico but would continue to sell him Omnitrition products.

The prospect of the resolution and more profits from Mexican sales really got Jim worked up, even though he and Jorge had come to hate each other for reasons that had nothing to do with business. He also agreed on principle to a non-competition agreement, but when the time came for him to sign the documents, he refused to sign.

Of course he refused. After all, he had already formed his new company!

ONE HAPPY FAMILY

In January of 1994, Bonner Geddes (the Special Master) arranged a meeting with Jorge Vergara. He had indicated to me that Jorge was interested in settling his suit, and Bonner had greased the wheels of the meeting by hinting to Jorge that we were ready to resume shipping product to Mexico. This was all occurring at the same time that Fobair had agreed to let me buy out his shares in the business for $500,000. It seemed that finally we were going to tie up all the loose ends.

Fobair and I went to the office of Mike Baggett, who was to meet with Fobair, Jorge, and other officials of Omni-Mex. When we got there we realized that Jorge wasn't any more ready to settle the lawsuit than we were, but after a lot of rehashing of grievances we decided that it was probably to both our advantages to do business rather than waste more money and time in the courts. The Mexican disaster had cost us big money and created a lot of bad feelings on all sides. But what was the point of cutting off my nose to spite my face? Restoring a business relationship with Omni-Mex meant potentially millions of dollars in profits.

Before the meeting concluded, we reached an agreement. Jorge would dismiss his suit, and Omni-Mex would receive an exclusive license to sell Omnitrition's products in Mexico. Fobair and I agreed that we wouldn't compete with Omni-Mex. Fobair also agreed that any company he might start would also not compete with Omni-Mex.

Later that night Fobair, Jorge, and I met for dinner to work out the details of what we had agreed to in principle earlier in the day. It was a good meeting. Afterwards, we all shook hands and, as usual, Jim asked me if he could borrow $100 for the dinner. Like always, I gave it to him.

Jorge's people were to prepare the "Settlement Agreement," which we all agreed to sign in the next week. I called home to tell Barb the good news and went to bed that night feeling I'd done a good day of business.

THINGS FALL APART

The next day, January 6, Fobair and I put our oral agreement into writing ("The Stock Purchase Agreement"). Fobair agreed to sell his shares back to the company, and we agreed to an even split of the profits, after costs, on all future Omni-Mex sales. All that was left was for us both to sign the Settlement Agreement on Jorge's lawsuit and the "Profit Distribution Agreement."

A week later we met at the office of Rick Graham to finalize the three documents. But sometime during the interval between our shaking hands on the deal and the time the papers were ready, Fobair had seen dollar signs. He had second thoughts about not competing with Omni-Mex, and he flatly refused to sign the Settlement Agreement. Because of his refusal to agree on the non-competition issue, the whole deal fell apart. Jorge flew into a rage, swore he would find someone else to provide him with products, and stomped out of the meeting.

But Fobair wasn't finished killing the deal. I had agreed to Fobair's price of $750,000 for his half of the company. The deal was that I would pay Fobair $300,000 at closing and then equal periodic payments. Fobair had placed his stock in escrow, for the purposes of this sales arrangement, with the understanding that when the note payments were complete, he and I would issue instructions to the escrow agent to release the stock to me.

As it turned out, even though all payments would be made, Fobair ultimately refused to issue instructions to release the stock.

DURK AND SANDY GET INTO THE ACT

On January 12, Fobair gave me a letter from Durk Pearson and Sandy Shaw in which they claimed that Omnitrition had violated their licensing agreement and noted that Durk and Sandy were looking forward to doing business with Fobair's new company. It also noted that new contracts would be required of both Omnitrition and Fobair.

This letter hit me like a bombshell. It was the first I had heard about any alleged noncompliance, and certainly the first I had heard that Fobair had a new company and that Durk and Sandy were cozying up to him. This letter had been sent only to Fobair, and Fobair had waited to show it to me at this critical moment. But that wasn't all. That same day I received a letter from Durk and Sandy putting Omnitrition formally in default and demanding a revised contract with Omnitrition that would allow them to license their revised products to other companies, provide for a shorter contract term with us, and require $1 million in liquidated damages.

They demanded that I agree to all these terms in writing.

I realized at this point that Fobair's goal was not merely separation from Omnitrition, but its destruction. As things stood at that moment, Omnitrition would not be selling product to Mexico, thanks to Fobair. Now, it seemed, the two scientists were using a phony noncompliance claim to strong-arm an increase in their percentages. Clearly, these were increases Omnitrition could hardly afford. I believed I had Fobair to thank for this maneuver too.

I was roaring mad now and not about to be blackmailed by Durk and Sandy, who seemed to be using the dispute between Fobair and me as an opportunity to line their loincloths. I told them what they could do with their revised agreement, and they then claimed they were going to terminate their licensing agreement with us.

Meanwhile, Fobair had more tricks up his sleeve. Under the Stock Purchase Agreement, I had released Fobair from his non-compete agreement with Omnitrition, permitting Fobair to sell Omnitrition's product line, but under a different brand name. I also had agreed to let him purchase, for a limited time, as much inventory as he desired from Omnitrition at wholesale cost. I did this not because I was a nice guy, but because I believed honest competition was good and that it would take several months for Fobair to get his company operating. Besides, I believed that on a level playing field Omnitrition could beat out any company Fobair could start.

Fobair called his new company Life Extension International (LEI). In doing so, he was capitalizing on the reputation and clientele of an existing organization, the Life Extension Foundation, a non-profit, tax-exempt organization headquartered in Ft. Lauderdale, Florida, that for some time had been conducting laboratory research and experiments in "life extending" products and some after-death preservation systems. Some of this was pretty dubious stuff. Under the law, the Foundation was not permitted to make health claims about its product. However, it did receive royalties through its "affiliates"—for-profit corporations manufacturing and distributing health products.

I'm not sure just what kind of deal Fobair cut with Life Extension Foundation, but knowing him as I do, it would allow him to pass off whatever product he peddled as having the Foundation's blessing. In any case, he wasn't satisfied with riding on the Foundation's credibility. He managed to make Durk and Sandy an offer they couldn't refuse. Then, they all went to work in coercing our remaining Omnitrition distributors into affiliating with LEI instead.

THE BIG LIE TECHNIQUE

During the last half of 1994, Fobair and his allies began a systematic program of intimidation and slander, aimed at destroying Omnitrition. The old lies were spread once again—that Omnitrition was going bankrupt, that it had ties to the Mafia, and that distributors' commissions were being wrongfully withheld. They even claimed that Omnitrition products were life-threatening and that Omnitrition executives (including me) were convicted criminals.

The fact that some of these statements were contradictory (Mafia-funded organizations don't usually go bankrupt, and his company was buying from us the products they claimed were dangerous!) didn't bother Fobair and company. The bigger the lie, the more believable it was—at least to some people. This was a hard time for the company and me. Once again, we were forced to take Fobair to court.

The problem with suing LEI was that Fobair's company existed largely on paper. Profits were yet to roll in, and there was no guarantee that we'd be able to recover damages, even if we won in court. So we also sued Durk and Sandy for defamation, attempting to get a restraining order that would prevent them from continuing to spread lies and harass Omnitrition distributors and customers.

The lawsuit languished in the courts but ended at last. Fobair and his allies backed off. LEI failed, even after Fobair's distributors put up their own money to found the company, and he went his own way into a series of largely unsuccessful businesses. We won our lawsuit against Durk and Sandy.

A chapter in my personal history and Omnitrition's was finally closed.

Chapter 17

~

The Case of the Vanishing Verdict

I GUESS I'VE BEEN LUCKIER IN LOVE THAN IN LAWYERS. When I bought out Jim Fobair in 1994, Omnitrition was involved in no less than twenty-eight lawsuits, most of them related to the buyout. That's a lot of fees—and a lot of lawyers collecting them. To date, I estimate it's something like $16 million we've paid them. But it's more than that. A lawsuit is one hell of a distraction when you're trying to build a business. Especially when there's no upside.

I've spent my time in courts, and it's not my natural habitat. That's what lawyers are for. It's their country. They know the legal lingo, and they know what the fine print of contracts is supposed to say. Yet, somehow, I often managed to hook up with law firms that botched deals, overcharged, or created more problems than they solved. Maybe it was because neither my partners nor I had any legal background and were therefore easy prey for bloodsucking lawyers. Maybe it was because, being a small-town boy, I just trusted people. In Salineville back in the 1950s, a man's word was his bond. Trusting your neighbors was a way of life. Nowadays in the big city you have to get it in writing, make sure it's witnessed, and then stand by for lawyers to beat each other up over what it meant. I think everyone needs one lawyer just to protect himself against other lawyers.

These days you have to watch your back twenty-four/seven.

< 111 >

LEGAL MALPRACTICE

Suing lawyers for professional malpractice is a lot like suing doctors. The profession tends to close ranks and protect its own.

We found that out the hard way. We'd had to go to court before with attorneys on billing issues. Each time we settled our problems with them out of court, and didn't receive much for our efforts. So I wasn't anxious to get into another knock-down-drag-out with another law firm, especially Gardere & Wynne, which was one of the most powerful law firms in the state of Texas. On the other hand, I felt that Omnitrition had gotten much less than it paid for with Doug Adkins (a partner at G&W) and Jane Ferguson, his successor as our in-house counsel. Major problems had been brewing for some time. Finally, things just boiled over.

BACKGROUND TO BATTLE

Doug had been Omnitrition's corporate counsel and an officer in the company since 1990. We were not only business associates; we had become friends as well. We'd gone fishing, and our families had taken vacations together. On a couple of occasions we went with him and his wife to his church, where Doug was a deacon. His church was one of the largest in Dallas, and Doug was considered a pillar of the community. But things began to sour when Doug started offering conflicting legal advice, telling Jim Fobair one thing and me something different. Needless to say, these serious actions prompted us to find new corporate counsel.

Jane Ferguson was a slender, red-haired woman who had been our in-house counsel during most of the Mexican fiasco and had been highly recommended for the job by Doug Adkins. She and Doug were good friends, and during the period of her employment with us she worked very closely with him. I thought she was more loyal to him than she was to Omnitrition. I was sure she tried to cover herself and Doug for their handling of negotiations with Jorge Vergara. After we

fired Jane, she became a partner at G&W. This only confirmed my suspicions about their relationship while she was working for us.

Our new attorneys—Scott Levine, Mike Betz, and Baxter
Banowsky—were energetic and hungry young lawyers who had
recently started their own law firm. They were definitely not part of
the Texas "old boy" network. The first and maybe toughest assignment we gave them was to sue Doug Adkins and his firm for negligence and breach of contract. We also named Jane Ferguson in the
lawsuit.

While G&W was working for us, the firm collected nearly $1.5
million in fees for their services. The Mexican fiasco was their worst
offense. Despite the so-called expertise and due-diligence they claimed,
we got bad advice from the beginning. As a result, Jorge eventually
seized control of Omni-Mex, we were ultimately forced out of Mexico,
and we lost our entire investment in that country, not to mention sub-
stantial future profits. In addition to that, Doug Adkins failed to
inform us of the potential sales tax and other liabilities, legal and
financial, that existed when Jim Fobair and I were buying out Charlie
Ragus in 1992. These proved to be in excess of $3 million.

And finally, during my dispute with Jim Fobair, Adkins often
played both sides of the fence to his own advantage, making the problems between us worse. After Adkins withdrew as legal counsel, he
purchased a controlling interest in another multilevel marketing company and used confidential information he had gained while working
for Omnitrition.

WE GO TO COURT AGAIN

On December 29, 1994, a letter was sent by our new attorneys
to G&W detailing our complaints and demanding compensation for
our losses, actual and prospective (a whopping $10 million by our
conservative estimation). The letter went unanswered. Big surprise!
So, in January of 1995, we began a legal process that would take
three years before it was resolved. We sued G&W for negligence and

breach of contract. They countersued for close to a quarter million in what they alleged were unpaid fees, but to us were excess charges. These I wasn't about to pay. I had already paid way too much!

The battle lines were drawn.

G&W probably thought the case would be easily defended. After all, our lawyers were new kids on the block, without the tie-ins with the Texas "old boy" network that greased the wheels of most litigation. They also knew that our earlier problems with lawyers had always been settled before trial. But they were in for a big surprise. Baxter Banowsky and Scott Levine might have been young, but they were smart, aggressive, and, most importantly, prepared. They researched our case for months, then presented the court with a mountain of exhibits—correspondence, bills, depositions—hard evidence of what G&W had done, what they hadn't done, and what they charged.

When the trial finally got underway, G&W's lawyer tried to convince the jury that our claim wasn't anything more than a nuisance suit, a waste of their time and the court's. They belittled my lawyers and me, claiming that we were just looking for someone else to blame for financial problems that we ourselves had caused. They dragged out the record of our earlier lawsuits against other lawyers and argued that in the Jorge Vergara matter I had been fully informed that Omnitrition didn't own a majority interest in Omni-Mex. They implied that we were conspiracy-mongers looking for money or somebody to blame for our own dumb business decisions.

Despite the G&W smoke screen, our case got even stronger when their own witnesses were on the stand. Jane Ferguson's testimony was particularly shaky. She testified under oath that she had informed me that we didn't own the majority of shares in Omni-Mex. But then we furnished the court with a document she had signed herself stating explicitly that we did own the majority of shares. Was she wrong or was she merely confused? For a lawyer who was supposed to be doing her job, it was bad news either way.

Naturally, Doug Adkins testified too, but he sometimes seemed confused about the facts, perpetuated the official line of his own attorneys that he was the victim of a disappointed client, and generally tried

to bluster his way through his testimony, confident that his big reputation and fancy suit would impress the jurors.

SWEATING BULLETS

I had been deposed for countless hours before the trial began, and
I always hated the process. It seemed to me that the lawyer for the
other side always started off by assuming, and implying to the court,
that you were a lying scumbag. That might have been his job, but so
what? It's still not a comfortable position to be in if you're on the
receiving end.

Neither Barbara nor I went to court prior to my testimony. It
wasn't a place I wanted to be. Our attorneys agreed it was best to
keep the jury's attention focused on the defendants. But Scott and
Baxter did a good job keeping us informed of what was going on at
the trial. Their daily reports were a lot like listening to a radio broad-
cast of a baseball game. It was all ups and downs. Sometimes your
team was ahead, sometimes behind. It all depended on who was at
bat, and what kinds of curve balls were being thrown. It was a rough
three weeks, believe me.

We chose Jarrett Lambert to testify as Omnitrition's corporate rep-
resentative. He was one of our original employees and became our
CEO in 1992. Jarrett was sharp and thoroughly in command of the
facts. The opposition grilled him for days, but he was prepared. He
told our story straight from the beginning, and didn't let himself
become rattled by tough questions. He made a good impression on the
jury, I think. Another good thing was that the G&W lawyers took
their best shots at Jarrett. That gave us a preview of what I would face
when finally called to the stand.

As I said, I stayed away from the courtroom, both out of dislike
for the setting and to keep myself focused on running the business. But
sooner or later I had to testify. After all, I was the one who insisted on
going to trial rather than settling as we had done in the past.

On the day I testified I found myself fielding a different set of
questions than Jarrett had. I guess the G&W attorneys felt the jury

wouldn't stand for a rehash of the same topics that had kept Jarrett on the hot seat. For several days, Scott and Baxter led me skillfully through my side of the story. Then, the G&W attorneys went to work on their cross-examination.

When you testify in court, you sweat bullets. It doesn't make any difference that you're the victim and not the defendant. As far as the lawyers for the other side are concerned, you're a liar and your testimony is worthless except insofar as it demonstrates your inability to tell the truth. More than that, they had painted me as a bungler whose misfortunes in business were my own fault. They wanted the jury to see me as someone looking for someone else to blame—like my hard-working, honest lawyers, the defendants.

I did my best to prove otherwise.

My philosophy is pretty simple: In court you take the oath and you tell the truth. But the disrespect and accusations are hard to take. Plus, the opposition always demands a degree of accuracy that few of us are capable of. Who really remembers the exact words of another person on such and such a date, or the date itself? That's why our own case relied so heavily on hard documentary evidence—what had been written in memos or contracts rather than something somebody said at a meeting or over lunch.

I guess I did okay on the stand. Our case wasn't about personalities. It was about lawyers and their fiduciary responsibilities to their clients. I tried to make that clear. We had shelled out big bucks over the years, and in the end what we had to pay went way beyond any attorney fees. Looking back now, I can hardly remember what I was asked or how I answered the questions. I know I sweated, and when the ordeal was over I felt a tremendous sense of relief.

THE JURY HAS ITS SAY

On July 21, 1995, the jury reached its decision. Oddly, it was a strangely illogical one. We had named both Jane Ferguson and Doug Adkins in our suit, along with Gardere & Wynne under the legal theory that allowed us to sue a negligent person's employer. Despite what we felt was compelling evidence and probably because the jury sympathized with a lone woman who often cried during her testimony, they found Jane Ferguson not to have been negligent.

But the jury's response to Doug Adkins was different. His slick, off-handed manner and huge legal fees had not sat well with the jury, made up largely of average Texas folks with an inbred suspicion of fat-cat, fast-talking lawyers and the big firms they worked for. Maybe they felt as we did that when a guy's charging those kind of fees he has an obligation to be careful for his client's interests. Doug they did find liable—and by extension—the firm he worked for. We had won.

It wasn't just a moral victory. The jury awarded us $11 million in compensatory damages. Punitive damages were to be considered the following day.

When Scott Levine called to tell us the good news, we were ecstatic. It wasn't just the prospect of collecting the damages. It wasn't just the satisfaction that we had taken on the Goliath of Dallas law firms and brought them down. It was relief. The trial had drained our energy and our finances. It had distracted me from my business and caused me to lose a lot of sleep. Now it was over.

Or so I thought.

THIS IS JUSTICE?

As it turned out, we had a lot less to celebrate than we thought. The next morning, Barb and I were sitting at the kitchen table in our home in Indian Wells, California, talking about the case. It was about eight o'clock in the morning, and we were still riding high from our victory of the night before.

Then the phone rang. It was Scott. I knew at once something was wrong. I could tell it in his voice, which had that I-hate-to-tell-you-but tone you can always detect just before the bad news slaps you in the face. Scott said, "Roger, you've got a decision to make, and you've got to make it right now." To Barb, who had gotten on the phone too, Scott said, "Remember, I'm your friend first."

Scott dropped the bomb, and it was a big one. He said Judge Hall had called Baxter and him into his office early that morning and told them that he had learned the jury had been exposed to some document or paper they shouldn't have seen. The judge never said what the offending document was, or how he had found out there was such a document, or why the document should have required a mistrial. But that's exactly what he said would happen if the parties didn't settle the case right away. A mistrial! That meant we'd be back to square one. It made me sick to think of it.

The judge had told Scott he could probably get us a settlement from G&W, but he needed to have the parties sign off on the deal as soon as possible. That's the decision I had to make, whether to okay a settlement or face a mistrial. I wasn't allowed to sleep on it. I had to decide right then and there on the phone.

Whatever the judge thought of this settlement, it left Barb and me fit to be tied. To us, the "victory" of the day before was like winning a gold medal at the Olympics and then not only having it stripped from us, but having the news that we had won suppressed too.

To this day, I can't figure out why Scott and Baxter thought the settlement was a victory for our side. For me, it was a cruel defeat. After all, the jury had spoken. Those folks sat through three weeks of complicated testimony and had agreed with us that we had been the victims of fraud and malpractice. That very day the jury should have been considering punitive damages. From those we might have gotten a good deal more than the $11 million the jury had awarded us in compensatory damages.

But none of that was to be.

Our judge, Judge Gary Hall, was very persuasive. Lawyers who don't go along with the judicial "flow" in Texas may find themselves at a considerable disadvantage next time they appear in that judge's court—if they're lucky enough to have a next time. Our lawyers—Baxter and Scott—never admitted to having been intimidated in that way by the judge. But I knew they were. Omnitrition had helped them get started as a firm, but the law was their livelihood and Dallas was where they practiced. However they felt about it personally, the judge had made them an offer they couldn't refuse.

The verdict had sent G&W's attorneys into a state of shock. They had obviously put a lot of faith in their trial strategy of dismissing our complaint as frivolous. They probably thought they had the jury in their pocket. To this day, it remains a mystery why Judge Hall insisted on the settlement. It didn't make sense to me then, and it doesn't make sense to me now. I, of course, have my own very strong opinion as to the reason, but what do you think? I bet your opinion is the same as mine! After all, they had a lot to lose. Not just the $11 million, but the possibility of punitive damages that might go through the roof.

Of course they knew they could have appealed the verdict and award to a higher court. They could have kept the case in litigation for another half-dozen years and maybe might have won in the end. But there was one thing they weren't willing to risk. That a major law firm like G&W had been found liable for negligence and breach of contract would have been front-page news in Dallas. Only a settlement would prevent that from happening.

Meanwhile, Scott was waiting for my answer. My back was against the wall. I said yes, although it galled me to do it.

And, as is usual in "out of court" settlements, none of the parties afterward could discuss the case. Not the $11 million, not the negotiations. As for the jury's verdict, it simply vanished. The only public acknowledgment of the verdict was a short article that appeared in the *Texas Lawyer* a few weeks after the trial. For the record, I quote it here:

THE DISAPPEARING VERDICT

Carrolton-based Omnitrition International won an estimated $11 million verdict in a negligence and breach-of-contract suite against **Dallas' Gardere & Wynne** July 21. At least, that's what several jurors say they remember. It seems 68th District Judge Gary Hall never entered the verdict into the record, and the jury charges disappeared by the time the parties settled the case for a confidential sum July 22. Unlucky

Gardere is the fourth firm Omnitrition has fought with over service and bills, but the first it has "won" against in court. Omnitrition, a network marketing company that distributes dietary supplements, has settled fee disputes before trial with Dallas' **Bickel & Brewer** and **Graham, Bright & Smith,** and San Francisco-based **Brobeck, Phleger & Harrison** in the past. Omnitrition filed the suit against Gardere and partners **M. Douglas Adkins** and **Jane Ferguson,** formerly Omnitrition's in-house lawyer, in January 1995, faulting them for not protecting the company from a securities suit filed against it in 1992, botching a stock transfer with its former affiliate Omnitricion de Mexico and facilitating a split among the company's partners. Gardere filed a counter claim for $258,000 in unpaid fees. Neither Omnitrition's lawyers, name partners **Baxter W. Banowsky** and **Scott D. Levine** of Dallas' **Banowsky, Betz & Levine,** nor **Mark T. Davenport,** a name partner in Dallas' **Figari & Davenport** who represented Gardere, will discuss the verdict or the settlement.

Texas Lawyer
July 27, 1998

I've often wondered about Judge Hall. In court, he had seemed like a fair judge. When I was on the stand testifying, he was attentive and courteous. Why wouldn't he let us have the victory? I have my suspicions. It bothered me that this "document" the jury was supposed to have seen was never identified. It bothered me that it was never explained how the jury had seen it, or exactly when it was discovered or by whom, or what it contained that might have been thought to influence the outcome of the trial. Pardon my paranoia, but the sudden and unexplained appearance of this mysterious "document" seemed awfully curious.

THE AFTERMATH

Years later, while writing this book, I made an effort to contact some of the jury, just to get their impressions of the case. The response of one juror was typical—she said she preferred not to be interviewed. She said the trial had left a bad taste in her mouth after the jury's verdict was ignored.

Who can blame her? She sat through the trial for three weeks, listened to the mountain of complicated evidence, and arrived at a verdict only to see it tossed in the wastepaper basket.

We went to court in search of justice and got kicked in the butt by the very system we put our faith in.

Chapter 18

~

Ephedra Wars

AFTER THE DEEP DISAPPOINTMENT of the "settlement," I was determined not to become my own worst enemy. The problem with lawsuits is that they keep your mind riveted on the past. I had learned a long time ago that success—in your personal life or in your business—is about the future. I had a business to build, a future to shape. It was time to move on.

During the next few years, Omnitrition continued to expand and prosper. Looking back to the nineties from the perspective of the twenty-first century, I am proud of the company's successes, especially in light of all the distractions, obstacles, and challenges. In its first eight years, Omnitrition racked up more than $287 million in total sales. Of that, $176 million was paid out to distributors in the form of commissions, royalties, and bonuses. That's sixty-one percent! But our growth wasn't just about money. It was about people. Our network of distributors was growing. We were expanding into new territory and helping more and more people run their own business and improve their lives.

During this time, I was as busy as I ever was. We were doing Rookie schools for new supervisors and conducting business opportunity meetings in people's homes all over the country. I wasn't living in my car or sleeping on couches like in the old days, but I saw a lot of hotel rooms and airports. I found the face-to-face contact with new distributors as exciting as ever. I never got tired of spreading the word because I knew it wasn't just about selling product. It was about changing lives, and I could see that my audiences were as excited as I was.

< 123 >

I had always believed that Omnitrition should bring only the best nutritional products to customers—the best that science could invent or that could be discovered in nature. During the first years of the company—and before their love of money outweighed their love of science—our dynamic duo, Durk Pearson and Sandy Shaw, gifted us with their extensive scientific background as nutritional scientists. They also shared with us their interest and research in herbs and other natural substances. One of these was the herb ephedra.

EPHEDRA—WHAT IS IT?

Ephedra—the herb the Chinese call Ma Huang—has been used in Chinese medicine for over 5,000 years. But it wasn't anything Aunt Glad had in her bathroom when I was growing up in Salineville, even though it had been available in Germany since 1896 and recognized in this country in 1926.

In 1992, we began distributing a new product that combined ephedra with caffeine and other nutrients as part of Omnitrition's weight-loss/weight-management program. The ephedra-caffeine combination was the result of research done by Dutch scientists.

Our ephedra product was an immediate success. Incredible testimonials from our distributors and customers using the product came flooding in. Barb and I used it ourselves, as we used all of our products. We were sure we had a winner. People were losing weight and feeling great.

But as always seems to happen, nothing draws fire like success. Look at it this way, here you have a low-cost, time-proven natural ingredient that actually helps people. The problem is, it's not produced or marketed by the big drug companies that have a vested interest in Americans being sick. Nor is it approved by the Food and Drug Administration (they only approve drugs), the supposed gatekeeper of America's health, who too often, in my mind at least, spends more time in the pockets of the drug companies than in serving the public. Companies like ours that distribute natural products are a threat to the dominance of the big drug companies. The FDA is *their* friend, not ours. Here's what happened to us.

First, let me give you some astonishing statistics. Americans spend well over $2 billion a day on health care products. They do this in an effort to deal with serious health issues such as diabetes and cancer, but also to improve complexions, lose weight, or achieve better muscle tone. Supplying their needs is the American drug industry, a multibillion-dollar operation. And however you cut it, these companies are in business to make money, not to promote the general welfare. They have big corporate offices to maintain and shareholders they have to report to. They spend millions upon millions a year advertising their products and in product development. As a result, Americans are the biggest pill-popping society the world has ever seen.

Too bad it can't be said that we're the healthiest.

For the most part, the drug industry makes products for the sick. The more sick people, the bigger and better the market. Healthy people don't need drugs. The increasing popularity of natural products— herbal products—is not so much designed to heal the sick as it is to keep people well. These products aren't available through the drug companies, so you have what the drug companies see as unhealthy competition.

The FDA serves a worthwhile role in protecting public safety against fraud and contamination, of which there would probably be plenty if the FDA didn't exist. But sometimes their regulations can be too restrictive and their vision too narrow. They admit in their Recommended Daily Allowances that the healthy human body needs certain minimal levels of vitamins and other nutrients. Yet when a company attempts to market the same type of vitamins and nutrients commonly found in the foods we eat, the FDA wants to classify the product as a drug. What do they want to do, reclassify bananas as drugs? And at the same time they insist that when an herb or vitamin supplement makes a curative claim it becomes a drug. New drugs that cure disease are wonderful, but so are natural and synthetic nutritional products.

Since the late 1980s, ephedra has been like a piece of real estate two countries are wrangling over. The FDA has been on one side, determined to show ephedra is harmful to public health; the millions of ephedra users on the other, equally determined to rely on our own experience and to take the management of our health into our own hands.

The flap over ephedra didn't surprise me. Remember, I had seen the FDA in action during my days with Herbalife, when the all-powerful government agency tried to morph a few deaths into hard evidence that Herbalife products were dangerous. I had seen how the so-called protector of public health could become a persecutor. And how this powerful government agency didn't always follow its own scientific procedures. I also saw how much the drug companies benefited by the FDA's efforts to suppress natural supplements.

This time, however, we common folks had powerful friends. In 1993, Senator Orrin Hatch of Utah and Bill Richardson, congressman from New Mexico, had introduced the Dietary Supplement Health and Education Act (DSHEA). The act aimed at giving the dietary supplement manufacturer, rather than the FDA, the responsibility for taking action against an unsafe dietary supplement product after it reached the market. This meant, basically, that manufacturers would not need to register with the FDA nor get FDA approval before producing or selling dietary supplements, although they were required to ensure that product label information was truthful and not misleading. After vigorous debate in both houses of congress, and a good deal of activity on the part of drug company lobbyists, the bill was signed into law by President Clinton in 1994.

Since that time, however, the war over ephedra and its active ingredient, ephedrine, has heated up. The FDA has continued to produce "evidence," they claim, of deaths resulting from taking the "drug." The problem with their evidence is the same thing that bothered me when the FDA attacked Herbalife products back in the 1980s. There were only a handful of so-called victims of ephedra out of the millions who had used the products and felt the benefits. If ephedra was dangerous to your health, why weren't more people dropping like flies?

For example, in a report published in the *New England Journal of Medicine* in 1999, researchers claimed that at least fifty-four deaths and about a thousand reports of "complications" had been linked to

ephedra since the mid-1990s. The subjects of the research were pur-
portedly "healthy young people," some of whom had been taking
ephedra for just days or weeks. There were 140 "users" who claimed
to have suffered complications in 1997 through 1999. From this small
sample, the researchers concluded that about a third of these were
"definitely or probably" connected to ephedra use, another third "possibly," and the last third with no connection to ephedra use at all.
From that the researchers further concluded that the dietary supplement posed a risk that far outweighed any benefits it might have.

Now, am I the only one who looks at reports like these and won-
ders why so many conclusions based on *probably* and *possibly* should
be treated as facts? Besides, let's assume that there were fifty-four
deaths and that they were actually caused by ephedra. That's about ten
deaths a year out of the millions of people who use the product.
Compared to the number of deaths from Tylenol, a common over-the-
counter drug, the number is quite small.

The authors of the article, commissioned by the FDA, admit that
about 12 million Americans used ephedra in 1999. How many deaths
during the same period might have resulted if those 12 million people
who used ephedra hadn't lost weight? Isn't excess weight considered a
health risk? Isn't excess weight associated with diabetes, hypertension,
heart disease, and a half-dozen other life-threatening ailments? I read
the other day that nearly 280,000 deaths are attributed to obesity each
year in this country. That's staggering. That's a worse health threat
than smoking.

Isn't it ironic that the FDA has created such a furor over the
ephedra herb and its handful of adverse effect reports, yet gave its
approval to the drug Phen-Phen and Redux, the supposed miracle
weight-loss drugs? I wonder what the death toll for these "acceptable"
drugs is up to now?

THE FDA LAUNCHES A MAJOR OFFENSIVE

In 1997 the FDA proposed a total ban on ephedra products used
in weight management, based on what it claimed were over 800

reports of adverse incidents. An "adverse incident" is the jargon used by the FDA to categorize just any complaint—everything from a heart attack to a skin rash—so the number of reports alone doesn't do much to indicate the size of the supposed problem. Keep in mind that the FDA didn't investigate and verify the reports. It only collected them.

The response of millions of Americans who used ephedra and had used it safely was almost instantaneous. Companies who sold products containing the ephedra herb, such as Omnitrition, and even Congress (where the nutritional supplement industry had friends) began to protest.

It was at that point that the government, so often on the other side of the fence, responded in a positive way. In May of 1998, the House Committee on Science requested that the GAO conduct an audit of the FDA's scientific basis for its proposed regulation, especially its cost/benefit analysis—that is, whether the risks of taking something outweigh its potential benefits to users.

GAO PUTS THE FDA IN ITS PLACE

You may never have heard of the GAO. It stands for the Government Accountability Office, and it's the investigative arm of the U.S. Congress. Its duty is to audit other government operations to make sure they're following their own procedures.

The GAO did exactly that to the FDA during 2000. Eventually, they issued a bad report card to the FDA. They found that the FDA had "inexplicably" used negative reports about ephedra in a way entirely unprecedented in their procedures, thereby violating the FDA's own policies! They charged the FDA with failing to confirm reports before publicizing them and stated that there was no scientific basis for the FDA's proposed ban on the use of ephedra products for weight loss.

All this is exactly what those of us who used the product had been saying ever since the FDA started its anti-ephedra crusade in 1994. Now an important agency of the federal government was saying the same thing, and it was getting the FDA's and the Congress's attention.

You've got to believe the FDA was embarrassed. On March 31, 2000, the FDA did something it doesn't do very often, if ever. It withdrew most of its proposed restrictions on ephedra products. We had won an important battle in the ephedra war. Our enemy, the FDA, crawled away with its tail between its legs.

MEDIA MISCHIEF

The problem wasn't just the FDA. It was also the media. As Richard Nixon once said, the media is America's worst enemy. I couldn't agree more. Although they claim to research their stories, it's incredible how often they just get their facts wrong. And when they're asked to correct their mistakes, they just bury a retraction somewhere at the bottom of page 37 or provide a small blurb at the end of the program. Case in point: the story on ephedra the popular TV show *Dateline* aired in April of 2000.

The segment questioned the safety of dietary supplements containing ephedra and strongly implied ephedra products were harming unsuspecting consumers. The show began and ended with the story of a New Jersey police academy trainee who had died from cardiac arrest. His death was blamed on ephedra. The producers went on to blame Congress for not regulating and the Dietary Supplement Education Act for the marketing of unsafe and poorly formulated supplements. They reported that Texas health officials had received over 700 reports of adverse effects, including at least eight deaths. Texas authorities were "concerned," the producers said, about the safety of ephedra products.

These misstatements and others were made on the program even though the producers had correct information available to them. For example, a noted expert in cardiac pathology had examined the police academy trainee's medical record and offered the opinion that his death was not related to ephedra but to arrhythmia arising from excess physical exertion. As for the 700 Texas reports, yes, these happened, but they were all related to a product called "Formula One." In 1996, the state of Texas took legal action against the company responsible for Formula One. In response, the manufacturer reformulated the product as part of the legal settlement. Since then, Texas has had only three complaints of adverse effects!

Finally, with respect to the DSHEA of 1994 and contrary to what *Dateline* producers claimed, manufacturers must back up all claims they make in their advertising. And the Federal Trade Commission has actively enforced the law. In fact, violators have had to pay multimillion-dollar fines.

So why had *Dateline* preferred fiction to fact, even when they had the facts available to them?

BAD NEWS SELLS

Well, let's face it—bad news sells. People will sooner watch a news program about a serious health risk than one that reassures them that everything is okay. Fear entices viewers, and more viewers means higher ratings and more advertising dollars. And it's pretty easy in our society to drum up a good head of fear.

I agree that there have been contaminated products and bogus cures over the years. Ephedra isn't one of them. Millions use it and have experienced its many benefits. It's just too bad the media doesn't focus on the good news. Instead, under the guise of "objective reporting," they ignore facts to alarm viewers and pump up ratings. *Dateline* producers had been given the names of experts who could testify positively about ephedra products. They chose not to interview those experts for their story. They didn't even acknowledge their existence.

SO WHERE DO WE GO FROM HERE?

In wars, you win some battles and lose others. During the late 1990s we seemed to have the advantage. Ephedra had not been adversely regulated, and it continued to benefit its users. Yet the FDA continued to wage war, not by hard scientific evidence but by innuendo, by periodically expressing its "concern," and by accumulating and encouraging "adverse event reports" that tried to blacken the reputation of ephedra and imply it was a kind of snake oil for the vulnerable and ignorant.

It just wasn't so. Scientific studies continue to show that consumers can achieve significant weight loss and other health benefits through the use of ephedra. Yes, any product can be dangerous—whether it's aspirin or common foods like strawberries or milk—if you're one of the few who are allergic. Any product can be dangerous to practically anyone if you take too much of it. If you don't believe me, down a couple of quarts of French Vanilla ice cream—brand of your choice—and call me in the morning. Believe me, you'll have an adverse incident to report, but who's arguing that ice cream ought to be banned or classified as a dangerous drug?

Ephedra is safe when it's taken in a way consistent with standards and when it's used for the purpose for which it was intended. Anyone who wants to confirm what I've been saying can read the scientific reports for themselves. Better yet, you can talk to any one of the millions of satisfied users.

Chapter 19

~

Summing Up

THERE ARE SOME TRUTHS ABOUT LIFE I think I've always known although maybe not always understood. At least not the way I do now. Some of them I learned while growing up in Salineville. They were what Aunt Glad believed, and she passed them on to me. They were things I was taught in church, and truths I learned the hard way on the school playground. They were values shared in that dinky Ohio town—values that made life workable and kept people decent. They were as much a part of the town as the big maples that lined Main Street.

Other things I've learned along the way were from my own mistakes and adversity. From being busted for drunk driving and going bankrupt during the recession. From being betrayed by supposed "friends" in business. I've also learned a great deal from my mentors, who were generous enough to share their wisdom with a bankrupt carpet cleaner and give me the opportunity to become something so much more.

And I've learned some of the greatest wisdom of all from my wife, Barbara, who's never been afraid to tell me exactly what she thinks.

These are the rules on which I've run my personal life and my business. I pass them along for what they may be worth.

FOR THINGS TO CHANGE, YOU HAVE TO CHANGE

The day I heard that quote is the day I started changing my life for the better. A lot of us spend a great deal of time blaming everybody else

< 133 >

for our problems. We blame the economy, or the government, unloving parents, or our own rotten luck.

Much of what we call "our problems" can't be changed, and it's usually futile to blame—period! No matter how bad our upbringing—that was then, this is now. If the economy is in a slump, there's not a lot we personally can do about it. And as for luck, well isn't that something we create for ourselves?

What we can change, though, is ourselves!

We can change our attitude!

We can make a new plan!

We can take responsibility for our life and make things happen!

But only if we decide that change is not just an option, but rather an absolute *must*.

The challenge is in knowing how to go about it. Change is scary. It puts us at risk of another failure. We wonder what people will think—and what we'll think about ourselves. To change, most of us need help. But it's not so much advice or therapy we need as it is courage.

Where do we find it? Usually we talk ourselves into it. I talk to myself in the mirror. I'm not embarrassed to admit it. I even recommend it. Look at it this way: Nobody knows you as well as you know yourself. Not your husband or wife, not your best friend, not even your shrink, if you have one. *You* know your dreams, your frustrations, and your fears. You know all your strategies of avoidance and how you distract yourself from doing what you know in your heart you must do in order to make things different. Dealing with yourself requires a little pep talk, a little self-coaching. Hey, you're looking at yourself in the mirror, talking to yourself. Do you like what you see? Are you satisfied with what you are? Sometimes courage demands that you learn how to kick yourself in the butt.

But the beginning of positive change in your life is accepting responsibility. You are at the controls. You can't control others, but you can control yourself. You have no one to blame but yourself. Remember, there are few circumstances in life you can change. The variable is you! That guy—or gal—standing at the mirror, talking himself or herself into making the changes necessary for a better life.

THE HAND THAT HELPS YOU OUT OF THE GUTTER IS CONNECTED TO YOUR OWN ARM

I don't know where I picked up that expression. Maybe it was Aunt Glad's wisdom, or maybe I just dreamed it one night after I had put the truth of it to the test. Most of us expend a lot of our available energy in counterproductive activity. Worry, for example. For many Americans this is practically a national pastime. But you can't worry yourself to success. You can't worry yourself out of failure!

For example, you can't pay bills by worrying about them. You can't grow rich by staring at the television. Watching television can become an addiction. You can sit in front of a TV wasting time by watching anything. Try turning off your televisions for a month. You'll be amazed how much more quality time you have to work on your business and spend with your family. Because when it comes to helping yourself it's not just vision that's needed or determination, it's time. You've got to learn how to use it productively. I don't mean simply that you need to get yourself one of those fancy planners in black leather or hire a personal manager to arrange your schedule. I mean you've got to take account of where your time goes, because that, my friend, is where your energy is.

So take inventory of your time. Not of what you planned to do during the week but where you actually put your time. Are you working to succeed, or just working? Sometimes even our few opportunities for leisure are wasted. Time is the most valuable thing we have because we don't know how much time we've got.

Finally, once you've dedicated yourself to being productive, set your goals. Remember, the most important thing about a goal is having one. Then go to work. I may be old-fashioned, but I believe in work. I think it's what made America great and what makes folks reach their goals. I think happy marriages are the result of hard work, and even raising children requires consistent effort.

If you think you're going to get from here—wherever *here* is— to somewhere else without work, you're living in a dream world. After all, the only place where success comes before work is in the dictionary.

NEVER LET WHAT YOU CANNOT DO PREVENT YOU FROM DOING WHAT YOU CAN

I picked up this expression from John Wooden, one of the best basketball coaches of all time and a great motivator. It ties in with something I've come to believe. One of the best ways to get "can't" out of your head is this: instead of jamming the two words together, try saying *cannot* so the positive and the negative get full emphasis. Hearing yourself say, "I cannot..." should make you angry because you *can* do anything you want to if you want to do it badly enough.

The trick is to set "got-to" goals rather than "want-to" goals. Take the words *worry* and *can't* out of your vocabulary. Decide that you've got to take responsibility for your future and your family's future.

Here's a story that illustrates the point. A salesman wakes up on a rainy Saturday and decides to stay home. He tells himself it is all right to take the day off because no one will be out on a day like this. But across town, another salesman wakes up to the rain and says, "All right! I've got to get going. No competition today. All salesmen are home in bed."

If you think you can't, congratulate yourself. You will be what you believe you can be.

MANAGEMENT REGULATES, LEADERSHIP MOTIVATES

We're all leaders in some aspect of our lives—or at least have the potential to be so. Leadership isn't a big mystery, but it's amazing how many so-called managers confuse leadership with intimidation.

Giving orders is easy. Any idiot can do it. All you need is a big ego and a loud mouth. A certain job title can give you the idea that you're in control. That the folks below you on the totem pole are there to obey.

But the real leaders I've known in my professional life have been men and women who share their vision with those they lead and, in so doing, motivate them to do their best. Not because they have to but because they want to. If you're a real leader, you're leading the pack, not driving them in front of you like a herd of sheep.

SACRIFICE—IT SOUNDS HARD BUT IT'S WORTH IT

I don't take to personal sacrifice naturally. It never sounded like a lot of fun to me, and as a kid I guess I was more into instant gratification. Buy now, pay later. But I've learned that sacrifice is indispensable to personal and financial success. Basically, sacrifice means you deprive yourself of something now—usually something you really want or prefer, for something else, usually a later benefit.

So what does this trade-off require? Well, first, vision—you have to visualize what you *ultimately* want. (We usually know what we want *right now* easily enough.) Children are poor planners because they tend to live in the present. The more immature they are, the more *right now* is all there is. That's why it's so hard for them to wait for Christmas morning to open their presents, or save a candy bar for after supper.

With adults, it's different. Or at least it should be. Everybody should know that if you want to save a thousand bucks you're going to have to sock some money away and that's going to require sacrificing something you want to get right now.

The principle's the same with time and energy.

The biggest sacrifice is getting rid of the distractions in your life. It's easy to get distracted by well-meaning family and friends, by preoccupation with your real or imagined faults. Negative emotions like jealousy, resentment, and anger can consume us. Look at it this way: There are three parts to your life—spiritual, family, and business. You want to be a success in all three, because failure in one can affect the others.

What do all successful people have in common? They all have twenty-four hours in their day. We all have the same twenty-four hours! The key is what you do with those hours. That's where sacrifice comes in. Need more time in the morning to get the job done? Sleep an hour less. Need more time in the evening? Watch an hour less of television. Are those one- and two-hour lunches messing up your workday? Bring a sack lunch to work.

Time is the most valuable commodity you have. You can't save it. You can only spend it. So don't waste it.

DO THE RIGHT THINGS FOR THE RIGHT REASONS

I've been preached at plenty in my life and I don't know that it ever did that much good. But I do believe it's important to be a straight shooter, both in your personal and business life.

Omnitrition is based on integrity and hard work. On zero tolerance for unethical behavior. That begins with telling the truth—to your customers, to your fellow workers, to your family members. One of my favorite quotes is from Abraham Lincoln: "No man has a good enough memory to be a liar and a success."

That means that a person who tells the truth will sleep better at night.

LEARN TO SHARE

Our generation has sometimes been called the "me" generation, as though we're a bunch of self-preoccupied jerks who care only about ourselves. Maybe there's some truth to that, although I've got to say that in my life I've known a lot of caring people who really do think about others. Aunt Glad was certainly that way. All the people I've respected throughout my life were that way. They were all sharers.

Sharing is a solid principle in business as well.

Success in my business, multilevel marketing, is largely based on the principle of sharing. We teach our new distributors that if they want to be successful, they've got to help their downline become successful, show them the ropes, help them enjoy success. Why? Because sharing always rebounds to your benefit. If not sooner, then later.

Of course, in multilevel marketing you can see the results of your sharing in your income. If your downline makes money, so do you. If they don't, you don't. What a lesson in the importance of sharing!

The greatest satisfaction I've had in my business is in seeing the changes success brings to the lives of others. Not just in people losing weight and getting healthier or in getting richer, but in improving their lives on all fronts—spiritual, family, and business.

THE SECRET IS: THERE IS NO SECRET

People will sometimes spend thousands of dollars on books, motivational tapes, and marketing gurus looking for the so-called secrets of success—in sales, investments, and personal relationships. They'll use the fact that they don't know "the secret" as an explanation for their failures and disappointments. They are deluded into believing that somewhere, someplace, someone actually has this secret. If they can only find out what it is, then they will achieve what they want without effort, without sacrifice, without preparation—just because they've got this SECRET, this key.

But the secret is that there is no secret. If there were, I'd tell you what it is, not hog it for myself. Remember, I said I believe in sharing, but I can't share what doesn't exist.

Success can be simple—if you're prepared to make the sacrifices necessary to achieve it. It can be yours, if you're ready to plan your work and to work your plan. If you can find the courage to change and change in a positive direction.

Is the risk worth it?

You bet it is. My own experience proves it.

POSTSCRIPT

~

I THOUGHT THE BOOK WAS DONE. But then things started to happen over the next year or two. Which I suppose only proves as Yogi Berra once said, "It ain't over until it's over." Anyway, just about the time you think things are going to even out and all the excitement is over, new things happen. One major event was Omnitrition's move to Nevada. Another was coming close to selling the company.

NEVADA HERE WE COME

By the beginning of 2001, we were struggling to stay afloat. Things were so bad that Barb and I were putting our own money in to keep the company going. To the tune of $50,000 a month! At the same time, we were paying back taxes to Texas and California, another intolerable burden and the results of bad advice we'd had from our high-priced lawyers.

For a number of years we had had a distribution center in Reno, Nevada. I always liked the place. I mean, what's not to like? It's got mountains, it's got lakes, it's got clean air. And we certainly had motivation to move. We were tightening our belts as a company. The move to Reno seemed a step in the right direction.

But, first, we needed to get our most valued employees at the company office to move with us. So I went around the company to find out who on our office staff would be willing to make the move. I was talking up Reno, pointing out to them how the move would benefit us all—as individuals and as a company. I managed to generate a lot of

< 141 >

excitement. And I was really pleased when they all said they were coming with us.

Then, while we were packing things up, things changed. I don't know what happened, although I suspect there was some stuff going on behind my back in the office. First, our accountant wasn't coming. Then our purchaser. Another key person wanted an astronomical increase in salary to make the move. Gary Garcia, now our CEO and a close friend, was forced to take over all these jobs. In desperation, I called John Sison, my brother-in-law. John had been in Herbalife with me and was thoroughly acquainted with the ins and outs of multilevel marketing. He was also up-to-date on our company's problems. John was working in Virginia, running a carpet company that was doing all the installation for Home Depot. I said, "John, we need your help."

John didn't take long to think about it. Despite his own comfortable job and beautiful home in Virginia, he was willing to pick up and move to Reno. Once there, he immediately set to work solving some of our biggest problems. For example, we had a hard time paying manufacturers, and got into a contract dispute with one of them. We believed that the manufacturer had failed on his side of the bargain, and in retaliation he cut off our supply. It's hard to sell product without product to sell. We went to arbitration and, despite his having a flimsy case against us, he won! We were ordered to pay $90,000 (but settled for less), and at a time when we could hardly meet expenses.

This dispute wasn't our only legal problem. A guy came forward claiming he had used ephedra for fourteen days and developed a pancreatic infection. When he threatened to sue us, our insurance company caved in, settling the case for $75,000. This wasn't our money, of course, but with the settlement the insurance company promptly cancelled our liability insurance. Later, we found out that the guy was an ex-convict who made a living filing lawsuits and then settling them for a lesser amount.

Meanwhile, we were still struggling with sales tax liabilities left over from our years with Gardere & Wynne. California was the hardest. We owed them $7 million in back taxes. We got Texas down to a little over a million, and were paying them $20,000 a month. It was awful. We couldn't get ahead at all, and, besides, our profits were down. Something had to be done—and quickly.

MEXICO AGAIN

One day while I was worrying about the state of things in the company, I had a burst of inspiration. I called Jorge Vergara, my old Mexican compadre. I hadn't talked to Jorge since our dispute over the Omni-Mex shares. It had virtually deep-sixed our friendship. But since then I had followed Jorge's successes. He had become an extremely rich man, most recently the owner of a soccer team. He had also become a movie producer and a major public figure in his own country. His company, Omnitricion de Mexico, was now bringing in about $1 billion a year. But for all his success we still owned the brand names of the products he sold. And the license was shortly to expire.

After we exchanged a few pleasantries, I said, "Jorge, my friend, would you be interested in buying Omnitrition?"

It wasn't that I really wanted to deal with Jorge, but I knew he was the one man who could save the company. It wasn't just my own neck I was thinking of. It was also my employees and the distributors, most of whom I counted as friends.

Jorge acted interested in my offer and wanted some figures, but at that moment I didn't have them to give him. It was one thing to blurt out an offer to sell. It was another thing to figure out just how much I wanted in the deal. So I told him I'd get back to him—and soon. As it turned out, as soon as I hung up I regretted making the offer. Sell the company? What had I been thinking! Certainly there were other ways to keep Omnitrition afloat. So I let the matter drop.

About a year later, I was having lunch in Palm Desert, California, with a friend. Suddenly my cell phone rang. It was Jorge, getting back to me. "Hey, Roger. You still want to sell the company?"

When I got back home, I set to work calculating not what the company was worth, but what I needed. I knew I wanted enough to pay off all the company's taxes and other bills. Enough to settle the lawsuits and pay off the lawyers who were bleeding us dry. I also wanted a little extra for my retirement. I thought Barb and I deserved that. The figure I came up with was $8 million.

We agreed to meet at a hotel in Los Angeles. We talked. We agreed. The issue was to be how the payment was to be made. Although the company was no longer doing business in Mexico, we still had a stake in that country and elsewhere in South America. That stake was product names, which we had retained in the earlier settlement with Jorge. But Jorge's license to use the names was about to expire. This meant that Jorge could either buy us out, or he would be forced to alter the names of his products, an expensive and, for him, extremely inconvenient alternative.

So the deal was this: I would give him the names for Mexico and South America and he would pay me $4 million on the spot (it turned out to be a couple of days later). Then he would send in his accountants and confirm the value of the company.

With the $4 million, I paid off everything—taxes, lawyers' fees, lawsuits. Talk about a relief! We were still rebuilding sales, but we were debt-free, and the feeling was great. And we had a couple of million left over (before taxes!).

But the sale was never completed. When Jorge's accountants got back to me, the offer had changed. Instead of the additional $4 million, he came back and offered me $1.6 million.

"No way," I said.

"But, Roger, we can still negotiate."

He really wanted to keep me out of Mexico.

So the sale never went through. The good news was that I kept the company.

EPHEDRA AGAIN

On December 30, 2003, the FDA put out what they called a "consumer alert" advising the public to stop buying and using products containing ephedra or ephedrine. At the same time, the FDA notified manufacturers that it intended to publish a final ruling stating that dietary supplements containing ephedra products present "an unreasonable risk of illness or injury." This meant that ephedra would be banned sixty days after the ruling's publication.

Some wars you win, some you lose. Now it was clear that we had lost this one. After the long struggle I recounted earlier, the FDA finally had its way, despite the weakness of the evidence against ephedra and the testimony of the millions of users who had been helped, not harmed, by this naturally occurring substance.

What this meant immediately for us was the loss of one of our best-selling products. Or at least the prospect of that loss. Fortunately, we had a stockpile of product that our many customers could draw upon. In the meantime, we put our researchers to work to find an alternative product. We've now done so, and have great hopes for it, picking up where ephedra left off.

LOOKING AHEAD

As I finish this book, Omnitrition International is alive, well, and doing our best to provide people with the unique opportunity to become healthier and wealthier. I have overcome many obstacles and beaten a lot of odds to get to this point. In business, as in life, there is rarely such a thing as smooth sailing. I know that for my business and me our most pressing challenges still await us. As in the past, we will meet those challenges head-on. Although we've had quite a history, I know this was only the beginning. The future chapters of this saga are waiting to be written. I predict that we will not only survive, we will thrive. You know why? Because when your business, and your passion, is about improving people's lives, there isn't a force on Earth powerful enough to stop you.

HOW TO CONTACT OMNITRITION

Omnitrition International, Inc.
5595 Equity Ave.
Suite 500
Reno, NV 89502

Phone:	(775) 335-4700
Fax:	(775) 335-4740
Email:	info@omnitrition.com

For more information go to **www.omnitrition.com**

www.RogerDaley.com